ANTARCTIC ODYSSEY

ANTARCTIC ODYSSEY

IN THE FOOTSTEPS OF THE SOUTH POLAR EXPLORERS

ACCOUNT BY

Graham Collier

PHOTOGRAPHED BY

Patricia Graham Collier

Carroll & Graf Publishers, Inc.

NEW YORK

Carroll & Graf Publishers, Inc.
19 West 21st Street
New York
NY 10010–6805

First published in the UK by Robinson Publishing Ltd 1999

First Carroll & Graf edition 1999

ISBN 0-7867-0653-8

Printed and bound in the EC

CONTENTS

ACKNOWLEDGEMENTS

The great majority of evocative photographs used to enhance this book are the work of my wife, Patricia. While I was contemplating and dreaming and scribbling the odd note to myself, she was making the photographic record of all our Antarctic journeys – scrambling up 100-foot cliffs to capture the portrait of the wandering albatross on its nest, or perched some 800 feet above the Southern Ocean on a slippery 45° slope to catch light-mantled sooty albatrosses winging home. As a geologist she also tutored me well on volcanoes, magma and tuff, on metamorphic rock and on the geological implications of glacial movement. And it was solely due to her initiative that these lengthy travels came about. In addition, she has built up over the years an excellent and comprehensive library of all things Antarctic – a source providing both pleasure and knowledge in a continuing compact with the southernmost continent.

Inevitably, there were occasions when photography was not possible: the capriciousness of the region's weather saw to that. So we are particularly grateful to the skilled photographers who permitted us to fill the gaps with their own images. It is difficult, for example, to capture the sheer verticality of Peter I Island from its narrow beach – and few people have had the opportunity to get near the place to try. Warren Krupsaw's picture of the black, arching buttress at the island's northwest corner is the only one I know. I am grateful to him both for providing the photograph, which is now in the Scott Polar Research Institute in Cambridge, and for allowing me to have a drawing made from the original in order to show the buttress-tunnel from a "close in" viewpoint. Michael McCarthy – the well known landscape artist of the American West – made the drawing. Conditions approaching the Barne Glacier from the Ross Sea did not favour photography, so when I came across Neelon Crawford's striking photograph of this glacier front, I requested his permission to use it; I thank him for allowing me to do so. He has been photographing Antarctica under the auspices of the National Science

Foundation for many years, and his work is included in numerous museum, corporate, and private collections. This image was in his 1994 exhibition, *Ramparts of Ice*, at the National Academy of Sciences.

Colin Monteath's Antarctic photographs are known worldwide, and after twenty-three seasons in Antarctica his repertoire is incredibly extensive. He gave me free rein to select pictures from his library, at Hedgehog House, which would illustrate the text in places where bad weather had hampered our own efforts. In addition, his editorial advice on the first draft of this manuscript was instrumental in focusing my thoughts, and drawing my attention to factual inaccuracies. For ten years he worked with the New Zealand Antarctic Research Programme as Field Operations Officer, and more recently was principal photographer for the *Reader's Digest Book of Antarctica*. A mountaineer, he was the first New Zealander to climb the Vinson Massif, Antarctica's highest peak; he has descended into the crater of Erebus; and in 1979 he led the team to bring down the bodies from the DC-10 crash on Ross Island. Few men in recent years have adventured so extensively on this icy continent.

The name H.G.R. King is acknowledged regularly – one begins to think, inevitably – in many publications dealing with the Antarctic. As the former archivist of the Scott Polar Research Institute in Cambridge, he facilitated our visits to the Institute and looked after us very well on every occasion. His book, *The Antarctic*, is still, in my view, the best overall reference work in the field after twenty-six years.

Gerald Pollinger's patience in handling three versions of the original manuscript was finally responsible for its acceptance. For over fifteen years I have come to know the reliability of his support – a backing which I acknowledge and very much appreciate. And finally I must thank my daughter Ruth Crowther-Smith whose eagle eye scanned a messy manuscript and transcribed it all without blemish.

G.C.

Postscript

I have always found duelling with editors to be a battle of wits – vexing and exasperating as key words, sentences, even whole paragraphs, come under the axe. Not so with David Blomfield, who invites dialogue to bring about a meeting of minds to enhance the book. I am grateful to him for taking such a civilized approach. And to Jan Chamier, a sincere "thank you" for her patient way of resolving problems and dealing with inquiries: always charming and efficient at one and the same time.   G.C.

I wish to thank my dear husband for his great heart in following my dreams as well as his own, and for turning those extraordinary shared experiences into a moving and eloquent chronicle. I wish to honour, too, the memory of Robert Black, Professor of Polar Geology at the University of Connecticut, who instilled in me – a lifetime ago – an enduring love for, and fascination with, the wild, empty and beautiful continent of Antarctica. I offer these pictures in partial payment of the debt I owe them both and hope that, although the pictures are simple and understated, they have captured some of the genuine mood, mystery and loveliness of this wondrous place.

P.G.C.

LIST OF ILLUSTRATIONS

LIST OF MAPS
(drawn by the author)

THE ANCIENT MARINER

"The ice was here, the ice was there,
  The ice was all around.
It cracked and growled, and roared and howled,
  Like noises in a swound."

I was twelve when I first read Coleridge's *Rime of the Ancient Mariner* – that epic poem of the albatross, spirit of the Southern Ocean, slain by an ignorant seaman: a killing that brings the skeleton Ship of Death down upon the offender and his fellow sailors.

In imagination I saw the limp bodies of dead albatrosses; fog-shrouded seas, dangerously splintered with dagger-like shards of drifting blue-white bergs, and home to half-crazed, gaunt skeletons of men enduring extreme privation and despair: mental pictures that provided the vicarious and visceral thrills of perilous adventure, and fed a child's primal fascination for awesome, phantasmagoric shapes.

The image of the dead albatross, pierced by an arrow, held up for view by a wild-eyed sailor could not be shaken off. I wondered where it was that ice "cracked and growled, and roared and howled". I consulted books; I looked at maps; I decided that the ship must have been at least 300 miles south of Cape Horn, in the notoriously violent Drake Passage, perhaps to the west of the Antarctic Peninsula, perhaps even further south in sight of the continent itself.

I saw illustrations of icebergs the doomed vessel might have passed – some one hundred feet high, and ninety miles long – sculptured, beautiful, sinister and dangerously seductive; I read of ice shelves as large as France, of an ice cap 12,000 feet deep, of waves 70 feet high, temperatures –80°C and hurricane winds gusting at 100 mph. Such are the essential elements in as formidable a catalogue of natural horror stories as one can possibly imagine.

Over time, the fascination felt by the boy for the scenes that Coleridge had described deepened; and when, many years later, the opportunity to

sail south presented itself, I was off. Now the geographical scale of the continent became apparent, and I realized that in fact there are two Antarcticas – two sides of the continent very different in character: West and East Antarctica, according to their position on either side of the 0° line of longitude or prime meridian. Even now comparatively few people, scientist or simple traveller, manage to see the western, more accessible, side; even fewer are able to approach Antarctica's hostile eastern – and more distant – reaches. I was lucky enough to sail round both sides.

It is relatively easy to travel to the northern tip of West Antarctica known as the Peninsula. It is a voyage of short duration and involves sailing from South America via Cape Horn, across the Drake Passage in the South Atlantic – a one-way distance of perhaps 1000 nautical miles. It is more difficult, of course, to journey to the South Pacific reaches of Antarctica – McMurdo Sound and the Ross Sea – which lie some 2500 nautical miles south of New Zealand. In either case, sea and ice conditions may prove difficult. Summer weather on these western routes – from the beginning of November to the end of February – is unpredictable, but is less likely to be as severe as that pertaining on the Indian Ocean approaches to East Antarctica.

The difficulties in simply reaching East Antarctica from either South Africa or Western Australia – 3000 nautical miles on the journey out alone – are formidable. Such a voyage involves a much longer time in truly high seas, with the prospect of more rigorous weather and an ultimate encounter with impenetrable ice. This is ice which takes two forms: that which is fast to the land and can extend seaward many miles, known as fast ice – and that which is composed of large floes having varying degrees of thickness and compactness, free-floating over miles of ocean, and known as pack ice, or simply "the pack". A certain amount of such ice around West Antarctica will usually break up and drift away in the summer, allowing strengthened ships access to the land. But this is not the case around the coast of East Antarctica where even an approach to the shore requires a powerful working icebreaker, and actual landings can only be made by using helicopters.

East Antarctica does not usually warm up to the summer level enjoyed by the west side: strong westerly winds can persist throughout the year,

OPPOSITE: *"The Rime of the Ancient Mariner". Engraving by Gustave Doré*

pushing off the vast ice cap with refrigerator-like effect, thus nourishing the persistence of fast ice and pack ice alike in the surrounding waters. As a result, miles of deep fast ice remain in position, firmly locked to the coast and very difficult to penetrate; while the heavy pack can be blown from pillar to post – without necessarily breaking up – and turn up where least expected.

This book is based on the experiences of many journeys through the pack to the great icebound continent. It gives, I hope, some idea of the joy and terror it inspires. I hope too that it may inspire the reader to ponder, as I have done, the question posed by the French explorer, Jean-Baptiste Charcot, who made his last Antarctic voyage in 1908:

> Where does the strange attraction of the polar regions lie, so powerful, so gripping that on one's return from them one forgets all weariness of body and soul and dreams only of going back?

PART ONE

WEST ANTARCTICA

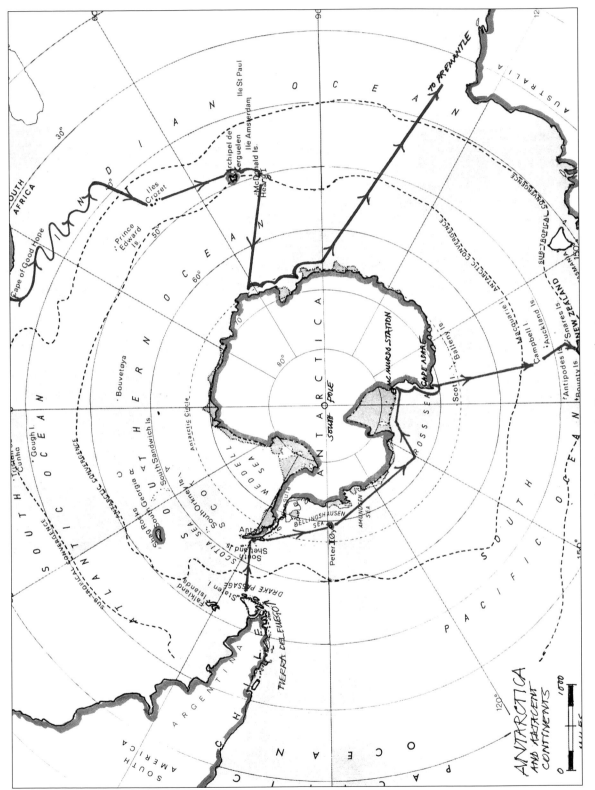

Antarctica and adjacent continents

1

POINTS OF DEPARTURE

PUNTA ARENAS, CAPE HORN AND THE CONVERGENCE IN THE
WAKE OF MAGELLAN AND FRANCIS DRAKE

Punta Arenas, Straits of Magellan, Beagle Channel, Cape Horn, Drake
Passage: wild, wild places close to the bottom of the world, these names
conjure up images of wind-wracked and icy mountain fastnesses, killer seas,
and primitive peoples. They are hostile regions, forever associated with the
legendary sailors who explored this maze of islands and waterways where
the Pacific and Atlantic oceans join forces around Cape Horn.

Ferdinand Magellan, a Portuguese captain in the service of Spain, was the
earliest of them: searching for a passage to the west in 1520, he discovered
the straits that now bear his name at 52° south. Navigating the waterway
westward – a tremendous feat, working an unmanoeuvrable square-rigged
ship against prevailing westerly winds up an uncharted narrow channel – he
thought the land to his left was the northern coast of Antarctica. He named
it Tierra del Fuego (Land of Fire) due to the smoke arising from the fires of
the primitive Ono Indians. Nowadays, for those leaving Punta Arenas at
night, the channel is lit by the burning fires of oil wells discharging gas.

Some fifty years later Sir Francis Drake sailed these waters in his
Elizabethan "cockleshell" of a vessel and was blown off course by one of
Cape Horn's notorious and vicious southwesterly gales – much of the way to
the Antarctic continent – and lived to tell the tale, so giving his name to what
we now call Drake Passage. Other pioneering captains and navigators
followed: Le Maire – who, in 1616, rounded the Horn and found that Tierra
del Fuego was an island; Captains Cook, Bligh, Ross, and Fitzroy of HMS
Beagle who took Darwin along as his naturalist – hence the Beagle Channel.

In southern Chile, roughly in the middle of the Straits of Magellan is
the small city of Punta Arenas – a bustling commercial port, just about at
the end of the inhabited world. Lapped by the waters of the Straits of
Magellan and buffeted by the violent winds and weather surging off the
high icy mountains of Tierra del Fuego, this far-south outpost, in its

magnificent setting and some thirty hours sailing time to Cape Horn, possesses an unexpected but genuine romantic appeal. It is home to some 45,000 people and is frontier-like in the rugged plainness of its old buildings and streets, yet it boasts some extraordinarily exuberant baroque architecture with domes, broken pediments, and bold cornices in the town centre that would not be out of place in far grander European cities.

Somehow the town manages to hint – like an experienced and well-preserved matron – that there's a rather sophisticated and pleasurable way of life available for those with discerning tastes: an urban maturity that springs from its proud history as a base for southern exploration and trade; from the "know how" gained in making the most of things when living in a far from benign climate, and remote from any cultural centre. Cut off from its capital city, Santiago, in the north by close to 1500 miles of untraversable mountains, Punta Arenas has had to develop its own ambiance. The result is a town which conveys to the traveller a sense of eccentric yet satisfied well-being – an unpretentious mix of homeliness and civilized values set in a landscape of wild and desolate beauty.

Now in midsummer the waters of the Straits on the left are almost Riviera-blue. To the right the immense, empty heath of wispy olive-green grass and scattered rock is sprinkled through to the middle-distance with colour: long-stemmed wild flowers – poppy-reds, cornflower-blues, yellows, whites – all swaying back and forth in the breeze.

Reflecting this exuberant sweep of colour, and standing in small patches of trim garden, is a long line of small box-like houses. These give little hint of the grander historic architecture to be found in the city itself, where the most remarkable building is the museum – a civic mausoleum into which every exhibit even remotely linked to the community's past has been placed for veneration. Rather like the town itself, the heterogeneous mix of objects and styles evokes an atmosphere of parochial self-involvement that seems out of step with the growing universality of the modern world's galleries. Yet it is appealing precisely because of this: it is honest – a catch-all collection representing the unedited life of a region apart.

The interior is a heady, paradoxical combination of rooms and exhibits. Classically proportioned chambers, well lit and dressed-out with baroque swags of satin falling from ceiling to floor, give way to smaller rooms – dark, shabby, mysterious and cobwebby places – charged with wonderful Gothic creepiness, and housing the most macabre and bizarre of exhibits.

The overall effect is like walking into a film-set for a dark and melodramatic nineteenth-century thriller. And it works. The museum invites one to prowl, to move expectantly from room to room wondering what could possibly come next after the two-headed sheep . . . and the bit of mylodon skin with its incredibly old covering of hairy floss. (The mylodon is a vegetarian giant sloth that lived millions of years ago, pulled down trees for food while sitting on its huge tail, and is thought to have been extant in Patagonia as recently as 10,000 years ago.) There is much enlightening information about the region's history: photographs of the original Fuegians – short, stocky and nude beneath their tent-like, animal-skin cloaks; many worthwhile geological, natural history, and "exploration" exhibits; and some of the worst, and funniest, examples of the taxidermist's art to be seen anywhere on earth.

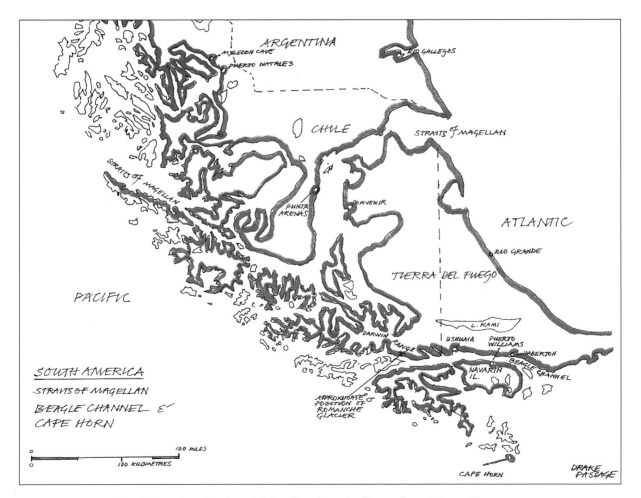

South America: Straits of Magellan, Beagle Channel, and Cape Horn

Magellan sailed out of the Straits on a day so calm that he called the wildest of the oceans the Pacific. Few others have been so lucky. Certainly Drake Passage – the Southern Ocean route to the Antarctic – well deserves its notorious reputation, traversing as it does that 600-mile gap between South America and the Antarctic Peninsula where two great oceans come together – the Pacific and Atlantic, hammering out their respective sovereignties before sweeping unchecked around the Antarctic continent as one momentum-building sea. Imagine Sir Francis Drake, in 1577 or thereabouts, in the *Golden Hind* – a square-rigged galleon of a mere 400 tons – running before a southwesterly gale, fighting a thirty-foot swell, and moving inexorably closer to the ice, thus inadvertently making the first Antarctic voyage ever recorded, though Hakluyt, Drake's chronicler, did not, of course, describe it as such. What a visual image it conjures up; and what terrors were experienced by those men who found themselves in these wild southern latitudes for the first time.

Our vessel is an ice-strengthened expedition ship of 2,500 tons, designed and equipped to withstand the rigours of the Southern Ocean, yet at times we feel as much a plaything of the wild winds as Drake and his *Golden Hind*.

A grim and utterly bleak sight greets us when the cloud cover over the Beagle Channel breaks, and Tierra del Fuego's dark, forbidding rock and tree-clad slopes are partially exposed – the snow-covered mountains and glaciers of the Darwin Range looming over the water. It is a grey, grey world, growing ever more menacing as the heavy stratus pulls away to reveal a jagged and dramatic line of peaks.

At the northern edge of the black depths seven hundred feet of blue-white ice cliff drop sheer and vertical to the water's edge – the Romanche Glacier. In staring upward from the narrow beach, the worm's eye-view of this tortuously twisted plunge of ice causes one to sway vertiginously, to lose the sense of solid ground beneath the feet, to feel as minuscule and insignificant as ants. Did I say seven hundred feet? From here at water level it seems a thousand at least. I try to imagine how small a man would appear to be up there on the sloping edge of the icefield: he would be a tiny figure – microscopic.

OPPOSITE: *The Romanche Glacier. "At the northern edge of the black depths seven hundred feet of blue-white ice cliff drop sheer and vertical to the water's edge."*
Photo: Colin Monteath

Only when one becomes accustomed to the scale of this visual phenomenon does the sound – hitherto merely background noise – manage to break through as a dinning roar in its own right. It is generated by a huge orgasmic jet of ice-foam water erupting from top-dead-centre of the ice cliff, falling and forking to form two waterfalls which slide down the steep face and plunge deep into the waters of the channel, creating a churning maelstrom of spray and wave.

If one visually climbs slowly and warily up the falls to the summits of the mountains above, the glacier itself comes into view: a huge body of ice, descending at a 50° angle to fill a broad saddle between two peaks – left and right flanks riddled with a maze of criss-crossing and razor-sharp open crevasses which swoop diagonally across the steep ice field from top to bottom. Deathtraps all.

A rasping tearing-at-the-air crack cuts through the general tumult, and a tall buttressing column breaks away from high on the precipice of ice and topples – a white cathedral in miniature – to splinter into glittering shards of glass as it falls, seemingly in slow motion, into the depths of the Beagle Channel. We are transfixed, incapable of movement. Senses and feelings are numbed by the sheer scale of these irresistible forces as one is attracted, like any moth to the flame, by that which is both beautiful and terrifying.

The first sight of the Cape Horn landing area is not reassuring. A slight swell is running in the South Atlantic from the Horn where a narrow kelp-streaming and rock-girt inlet gives access to a steep, cramped beach.

Fog and drizzle graze the rounded summit, lifting briefly from time to time to expose a wilderness of grey-green scrub and tussock grass – concealing the burrows of breeding Magellanic penguins, and permitting views at sea level of long dark fingers of water racing between skinny rock promontories, which grasp the island without mercy or remorse. Here, in the force of the flow, one sees for the first time the full power of the combined South Atlantic and South Pacific oceans – a run of sea which already, here at the Horn, may justifiably be called the Southern Ocean.

The ground squelches and sinks underfoot, peat-like bog not far from the surface. It is monochromatic desolation. It is the end of the world: the place where the shades of the dead in Greek mythology would gather to await Charon and his boat to be rowed to Hades – the land of the dead that must surely lie somewhere just across the water in Tierra del Fuego.

As if to dispel such feelings of dread, a tiny wooden chapel emerges from the mist, about the size of a ship's longboat and sited on the highest point of the island. Inside it is a quiet, holy place – or so I find it to be. In one of nature's bleakest outposts it is a symbol of a human religious dream, a spiritual refuge from a physically violent world – lending heavenly support to the few men of the Chilean navy who man the rock.

"Rounding the Horn": the phrase evokes pictures in the mind of vessels under sail trying to beat from east to west against the prevailing winds, to survive the ferocity of the westerlies rushing against them out of the vastness of the South Pacific – winds building, continuously intensifying, as they rush on their unimpeded race around the bottom of the world. Captain Bligh in the *Bounty* tried for thirty days to round Cape Horn – perhaps within sight of where I am standing – and enter the Pacific; like many others before and after him, he could make no headway. To the crew's relief he finally turned and sailed east, taking the westerlies in his sails to blow him across the Atlantic to South Africa, where he passed safely by the treacherously-reefed Cape of Good Hope, thus taking the long way round to Tahiti and the South Pacific. However, there were those historic figures who were lucky enough to slip through during lulls in the weather: Sir Francis Drake was one, but only after sustaining a hell of a battering. Before the opening of the Panama Canal countless ships were lost in these waters. Even the most experienced sailors, or perhaps especially the most experienced, grew anxious once south of the Falklands and heading southwest, ready to take in sail as they approached this barren outpost of land.

Without warning a bleakness of spirit abruptly descends on me – a mood of despondency at the sudden apprehension of the futility and inconsequence of human affairs in the face of such dark wastes of sea and rock. Reeking of melancholy at its best, and spitting malevolence at its gale-ridden worst, Cape Horn must surely represent the ultimate isolation and desolation. The Romanche Glacier fires the spirit, Cape Horn subdues it.

The relatively narrow channel between South America and the Antarctic Peninsula was caused by the breakaway of the Antarctic land mass from the Americas some fifty million years ago – a separation responsible for the ultimate glaciation of Antarctica, a once warm, tree(beech)-clad land.

Through it runs a body of water incorporating the force of three oceans: the Pacific to the west, the Indian Ocean to the east, and the Atlantic to the north. In latitudes 40°, 50°, and 60° south, this mighty oceanic force, having no substantial land in its path for thousands of miles, races unimpeded around the Antarctic continent building into what must surely be the most powerful, long-rolling swell in the world.

Some 400 miles from Cape Horn, we pass through the Antarctic Convergence. Generally recognized as the oceanic boundary of the Antarctic regions, this is an invisible boundary, but one which can be felt as a distinct drop in air temperature. A stream of water some twenty to thirty miles wide, it represents the region where the cold currents moving up from the south sink beneath and lower the temperature of the warmer water flowing down from the north. This ocean mix rings the entire Southern Ocean – some would prefer to say it establishes the northern boundary of the Antarctic Ocean around the continent – and follows roughly latitude 50° south in the Atlantic and Indian Ocean sectors, and 55° to 60° south in the Pacific region. Not only is the ocean's surface temperature affected, but changes in chemical composition are apparent at the convergence.

Just before we reach the Atlantic Convergence, the first icebergs appear. Small and irregular, weathered by wind and sea on their long journey from the glacier front that calved them they move steadily toward inevitable dissolution in the warmer northern waters. Biological differences in the sea's plant and animal life also occur, providing a richer harvest of food for all sea-going animals – pelagic birds being visually the most obvious beneficiaries.

Convergence, icebergs, birds – all are signs of the nearness of true Antarctic waters.

Birds: every hour of each increasingly long day they are with us. A panoply of birds. More birds performing more spectacular feats of flying than one would expect to see in a lifetime. Formations of black-and-white-checked cape pigeons fly undulating sea-level sorties. They are followed by southern giant petrels with their four-foot wingspan, together with the smaller storm petrels zigzagging across the sky, skimming the waves a fraction of an inch above the surface, one minute straight and level, the next making a startling 180° turn with a single wing tip downturned in a

OPPOSITE: *The Southern Ocean. "The most powerful, long-running swell in the world"*

90° bank and actually drawing spray from a racing wavecrest: a ballet of flashing scimitar-like wings governed by a wonderful aerobatic judgment. The larger petrels in particular can make a quick half-roll to level-out, a sudden soaring upward from the sea with no discernible stretch of wing or flick of feather – where they then stay, gliding, in full forward motion without any obvious means of propulsion. Breathtaking flying. One has to wonder at that small chip of a brain up there in the bird-skull, and the marvellous complexity of "wiring" that could produce such consummate aerodynamic performance.

And then, behind the bold and marauding petrels, are the more solitary-flying birds, higher in the sky at, say, three hundred feet – wandering albatrosses together with a number of the slightly smaller royal albatrosses, all maintaining a surveillance of their ocean territory – and no less riveting to watch, both by virtue of their great size and the arresting nature of their flying virtuosity. For if the petrels are the experts at close-in manoeuvrability, the albatrosses carve great spatial arabesques, wheeling, soaring, and gliding on air currents with what seems to be supernatural ease and grace – their ten feet or more of dihedrally-fashioned narrow wing giving an appearance of aerodynamic invulnerability as they sweep the sky. Possibly the albatross cannot match the tight turns and bursts of speed while poised on a mere wing tip which give the petrel low-flying supremacy, yet surely no petrel can out-soar, out-glide, or surpass the efficiency and artistry of the albatross as the long-distance maestro of the upper air.

Having made this comparison, I must then report that it is the kind of generalization which does not always hold. For when one sees a royal albatross suddenly abandon straight and level flight and spiral upward like an aerial corkscrew, it is with a certain measure of disbelief. And when the bird breaks abruptly from the updraft, appears to rake the leading edge of its wings backward about 25° while simultaneously pushing head and body forward and down, careening for the water in the fastest, most controlled, free-fall dive you can imagine – all of two hundred vertical feet at the very least – anyone who has ever flown will have the stick pulled right back into the groin at least halfway down in the bird's dive. But the albatross will

OPPOSITE: *The first icebergs at the Convergence. "Small and irregular, weathered by wind and sea on their long journey from the glacier front that calved them they move steadily toward inevitable dissolution in the warmer northern waters."*

have none of it. Keeps on coming, dive-angle and velocity unchanged. Only at the last minute, just a few feet above the surface, forward goes the leading edge of the wings, up come the wing tips in an 50° arc, the tail spreads, and with belly drawing spray from the wave, the great bird takes its catch.

You have to grab a quick breath at this: for you expect the albatross to lower its trailing wing-edges to act as flaps, spread undercarriage-feet forward as air-brakes, and land on the water. Not a bit of it: somehow conserving all the speed gained in its momentous plunge, this incredible aviator – without a single beat of its wings, or real break in the continuity of its flight – manages to pull upward, shape a perfect parabola, an ascending arc, the mirror-image of its line of descent. Up and up it goes, back to the wide reaches of altitude where, joyously and abandonedly, it turns to glide away, still soaring, to the north.

When one is in the presence of a solitary albatross – and particularly a wanderer, larger than the rest – aloof and extraordinarily beautiful in its own airspace, it is easy to understand how such a creature aroused strong feelings of a mystical sort among southern sailors – and this before any naturalist investigated the bird's way of life and told us about the solitary early years spent entirely at sea gliding and riding the air currents; or about the long wait for the onset of a breeding maturity that finally, perhaps after three years on the wing, would drive male and female to return to their natal island – yet even then merely as apprentices so to speak, as young performers of the elaborate courtship-dance-rituals which would be repeated for the next few summers: a way of creating a bond which usually lasts for life. And, bear in mind, the wanderer may live to be fifty. Small wonder that many professional observers of these birds are fascinated by them; that writers after Coleridge have been inspired to romantically invest these long-distance solo flyers with such powerful symbolic properties.

For myself, I suspect that no other bird in the world will ever command such a profound image of avian grandeur and presence.

Following the solitary bird through binoculars, mesmerized by the high figure-of-eight wheelings when it seems totally uninterested in the sea as a source of food, I have found it impossible to escape the feeling that this great ocean-going flyer possesses a rare aura of dignity and purpose in playing its role in the scheme of things, and is of a wise and gentle nature.

14

Portrait of a wandering albatross. "… it is easy to understand how such a creature aroused strong feelings of a mystical sort among southern sailors."

If asked to expand on such a personal opinion I can only say that I imagine its three-year quest on the wing over the Southern Ocean to be in the nature of a vigil – a watchful and formal ritual to which this glorious bird, obedient to some profound inner directive, is irrevocably committed.

More than once I have had the thought that it would be wonderful to be descended from the great birds rather than from the great apes.

2

MAROONED

DECEPTION, ELEPHANT, AND SHACKLETON'S
RACE FOR SURVIVAL

At Deception Island, the worst of Drake's Passage is behind us. Deception lies south and west of King George Island in the main South Shetland group at latitude 63° south, well within the Convergence, yet just outside the Antarctic Circle.

It is a creepy place – even a frightening one. What we call an island is, in fact, all that remains of a drowned volcano. To visualize it, imagine a volcanic cone sinking beneath the ocean to leave only the last thousand feet of its crater-rim – a caldera eight to nine miles across – above the water. At some point in time the sea breached the eastern rim, permitting the ocean to roll in and fill the crater, thus creating the relatively narrow but spectacular entrance opening known as Neptune's Bellows: near-vertical walls of dark volcanic rock, ice-girt and forbidding.

Deception Island is black and white; there is no colour, just thick black volcanic sand and dust, black tuffaceous cliffs and steep cindery slopes broadly streaked by snow-bands of dirty volcanic ash. On this particular afternoon, it is overspread by a slate-grey, heavy-hanging sky.

In Whaler's Bay stands a long-deserted whaling station, a forlorn relic of brutality slowly rusting away in this lost corner of the earth. On the beach the wrecks of old whaling longboats lie half-buried beneath volcanic debris sharing space with scattered whale ribs and vertebrae – and six or seven uninterested fur seals. Skuas stand like Roman eagles in puddles of black water at the base of dirty black cliffs. It is a seemingly ancient place – a tragic site in antiquity. The sands are littered with bones like a battlefield at the end of the day and one wanders about like Antigone searching for a brother, or a Valkyrie collecting the souls of the fallen heroes. In this place,

OPPOSITE: *Ice and ash, Deception Island. "It is a creepy place – even a frightening one. What we call an island is, in fact, all that remains of a drowned volcano."*

at such moments, it is as if one is staring into the very mouth of the underworld.

The whaling station was operated by the Norwegians between 1910 and 1931. Since then the island has been occupied by the Argentines, Chileans, and the British – all of whose scientific stations were hurriedly abandoned after a submarine eruption occurred in Telefon Bay in 1967. Volcanic activity is still very much in evidence. It is possible to swim in the caldera – undressing hastily on a black-sand beach with the air temperature about 35°F – and entering the water where a haze of warm mist hugs the surface: here the water temperature may exceed 100°. However, there is no transition zone between this overheated water and the water that surrounds it which is only a few degrees above freezing. The interface between is as thin and as sharp as a pane of glass. If one moves accidentally out of the area of thermal activity into the frigid water beyond, the pain is startling and intense, a harsh reminder that one's life expectancy in Antarctic waters is measured in no more than minutes.

Beyond Neptune's Bellows lies a narrow strip of beach known as Bailey Head on the caldera's ocean side. Here the coarse black and cindery cliffs rise steeply in a series of rounded abutments which are riven by icefalls spilling from the heights – cascades of melt water streaming over the black rocks and channelling their way across the narrow beach to the sea. And everywhere there are penguins – a huge colony of chinstrap penguins, so called because of the thin black line running down one side of the head, under the chin, and up the other side. Thousands of nesting pairs fill the beach to the north, while a continuous stream of birds comes marching round the southern headland. The main body parades like a platoon of helmeted guardsmen, but the stragglers keep to no formation and wander aimlessly over the rocks, stopping suddenly to stare into the middle distance, or to bend and peer myopically at something on the ground. Smaller penguins – which is to say all species save kings and emperors – present an awkward yet humorous picture when on land with their stilted and swaying walk. Yet in the water, which is their true element, they are as agile and elegant as seals.

To see hundreds of chinstraps surging toward the beach after fishing in

OPPOSITE: *Remains of whaling station, Deception Island. "… a forlorn relic of brutality slowly rusting away in this lost corner of the earth."*

Chinstraps at Bailey Head. "... the stragglers keep to no formation and wander aimlessly over the rocks, stopping suddenly to stare into the middle distance, or to bend and peer myopically at something on the ground." Photo: Colin Monteath

deep water is an impressive sight. At first, they appear simply as a line of long silver ripples disturbing the surface of the sea; then, as they close the distance, their fast and graceful porpoising action becomes apparent as flotillas of airborne bodies leave the water to arc briefly through the air, dive, re-emerge, fly, dive again – at what seems to be an ever-accelerating speed. Suddenly there they are in shallow water, where, amidst a flurry of spray, they heave themselves ashore with one final power-driven leap.

When one is wandering among such a mass of birds in a rookery, circling a maze of layabout seals disporting themselves belly-up, snoozing and snoring as they do when high and dry, the inner caldera's seeming world of the Ancients is gone. Weddell seals, fur seals, elephant seals and crabeaters sprawl and crawl, flippers moving desultorily to administer a half-hearted scratch here and there; some emit the odd hoot of protest as a neighbour drags itself half over them, seeking softer cushioning than that offered by the shoreline rocks. Several animals show severe scarring over

Weddell seal pup. "Weddell seals, in contrast, are generally placid and gentle creatures and will roll over on to their backs, regarding you with round and luminous eyes as endearing as those of a Labrador puppy."

their bodies – the results most likely of predatory attacks by leopard seals or killer whales. Nevertheless, *en masse*, they give the impression of a surreal graveyard of unburied giant snails – bulbous creatures that have lost their shells and are just on the verge of expiring.

In general, they usually take little notice of human intruders, which is surprising when you realize that fewer than seventy years ago their ancestors were clubbed to death on these very beaches to obtain their skins and oil. Even so, one must be aware that both fur seals and elephant seals can be aggressive and both species can and will inflict almost invariably septic bites: fur seals in particular tend to be testy and are remarkably fast on their flippers. Weddell seals, in contrast, are generally placid and gentle creatures and will roll over on to their backs, regarding you with round and luminous eyes as endearing as those of a Labrador puppy.

Seals swim desultorily in shallow water close in to the beach, and from time to time an individual seems to tread water and expose just its head. I am obviously the object of curiosity while walking around among the penguins, for an offshore fur seal pokes its head up out of the water and stares intently in my direction. Something about its newly visible profile – the manner in which the head is pushed horizontally forward, with the mouth slightly open – gives the animal the reptilian appearance of a leopard seal. It is an instant alarm signal: immediately every penguin in the water heads in panic for the shore. A second or so later they realize their mistake and, almost nonchalantly it seems, as if nothing untoward had ever happened, resume their normal activities.

The ocean-facing side of Deception Island is even more stark and uninviting than the relatively calm interior. Here, the very steep outer sides of the caldera are ringed at their bases by thirty-foot cliff-like outcrops of buttressing ice, deeply fissured, and alive with the constant roar of falling water. Streams race somewhere within this glacier-like fringe before finding some deep fracture, through which they are released as forceful mini-waterfalls to the black sand of the shore.

On this beach there is little or no shelter from the howling winds and pounding surf; yet, bleak and unprotected as it is, it is capable of supporting an abundance of life. Birds, penguins, seals – they all have survived the dreadful history of this place: the sealers and the whalers and the volcano with its suffocating ash and poisonous gases. They have ridden out the wild winter storms and dodged the hidden predators of this cold, black sea. Perhaps these are the true heroes of this desolate beach.

The name "Elephant Island" is deceptive for it suggests a rounded, elephantine hunk of rock washed by tropical or semi-tropical seas. Nothing could be further from the truth. For this island, lying northeast of Deception and the northernmost member of the South Shetlands group is no benign, maternal haven.

The visual prospect of the island is the very antithesis of elephantine rotundity. Here cliffs rise 2000 feet sheer from the ocean to end in high, cloud-shrouded peaks; and the sea-facing fronts of massive glaciers intrude between the headlands. Even in the summer months Elephant Island is rarely accessible to shipping. Situated as it is between the high rolling swells and strong winds of the lower Drake, and the fierce currents of the Weddell Sea to the east, the place is beset by a rough, oceanic-Antarctic climate, buffeted by strong winds and a fast-running sea. As the winter

Elephant Island. "… a place of awesome elemental grandeur and power."

pack ice breaks up and drifts north and west from the Weddell Sea, wind and current take it toward Elephant where it can collect – as iron to a magnet – for much of the year, laying siege to the land in the form of grounded icebergs or a jumble of pressured pack ice.

Elephant Island is a place of awesome elemental grandeur and power. Yet the island's place in Antarctic history is not based on its icebound fastness, nor the inaccessible nature of its cliffs and mountains, but on the role this lonely spot played in one of the epic stories of survival in the history of exploration, Sir Ernest Shackleton's ill-fated 1914 *Endurance* expedition.

Shackleton's plan was to penetrate the ice of the Weddell Sea, on the east side of the Peninsula, and reach a point offering the shortest access

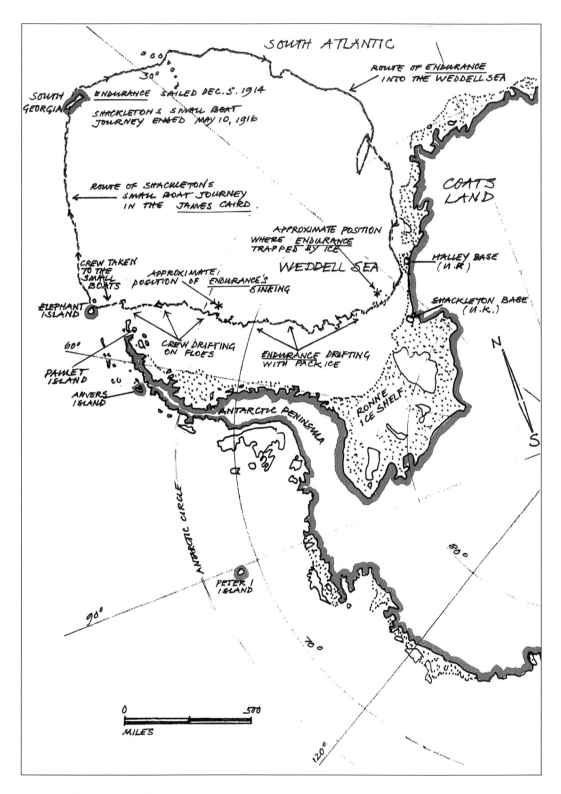

The Antarctic Peninsula and Weddell Sea: Shackleton's Endurance *expedition*

over the ice to the continental land mass. From there he would attempt to make the first ever crossing of Antarctica, heading to the Ross Sea some 2050 miles away via the South Pole. The journey was to be accomplished by a dog-and-sled party – five men and fifty-four dogs – and was calculated to take 120 days.

As things turned out, the land party never got underway. The summer pack ice that year was particularly extensive and dense – the weather, being unseasonably severe for the season, did little to help in the break-up of the pack. Shackleton spent five weeks seeking leads (lanes of open water) which would provide access to the coast of Coats Land. Finally, after a succession of blizzards and gales, a survey of their position on 25 January 1915 indicated that the ship was completely held by the ice: "The ice was packed heavily and firmly all round the *Endurance* in every direction as far as the eye could reach from the masthead." So reads the report.

There was to be no escape for the ship from this stranglehold. Firmly locked in the ice, she drifted about six miles a day with the pack for some 281 days until late October of that year – covering a distance of 1500 miles to finish 570 miles north and west from where she was first trapped. During this time the men hunted seals and penguins for sustenance. On 27 October it was obvious that she was finally being crushed to death by powerful pressure ridges in the ice, and that there was no alternative but to abandon the vessel to her fate.

Frank Worsley, the captain of the *Endurance*, described in his diary the events which forced the abandonment of the ship: "Two massive floes, miles of ice, jammed her sides and held her fast, while the third floe tore across her stern, ripping off the rudder as though it had been made of matchwood. She quivered and groaned as rudder and sternpost were torn off, and part of her keel was driven upwards by the ice. The shock of the impact was indescribable. To us it was as if the whole world were in the throes of an earthquake."

Camp was pitched on the ice, but it was not until 21 November, almost a month later, that what was left of the *Endurance*'s stern lifted into the air and the ship sank below the waters of the Weddell Sea.

It was when the floe beneath them began to break up with the approach of the Antarctic summer that Shackleton decided on 20 December to head northwest across the pack to Paulet Island some 350 miles away. (It was closer to their position than Elephant Island which lay 180 miles further north and west.) But after taking four days to travel just eleven miles through deep snow and rotten ice, Shackleton abandoned the hike and decided to take the chance of drifting north-northwest on a large ice floe. Together with the ship's three small boats – which they had manhandled over the ice to this point – the party of twenty-eight men retreated to a floe which, however, cracked under them during the night, necessitating a shift to a more substantial expanse of floating ice. This happened on 29 December 1915; they were now irrevocably committed to the currents and winds of the Weddell Sea.

The men had been camped on sea ice, on ice rafts, from 28 October and now, after the abortive attempt to cross the ice on foot, Shackleton's last hope was that the fast-drifting pack would carry them to open water where the boats could put to sea to reach Paulet Island. Unfortunately, the floe's drift was too westerly, causing them by 17 March to pass abreast of their desired destination by sixty miles. There was no hope of crossing the decaying sea ice to reach it and no open water that would permit launching the boats.

On 8 April 1916 misfortune struck again as the ice beneath them started to disintegrate, and their last floating home had to be abandoned. The expedition photographer, Frank Hurley, described what happened: "Shortly after 6 p.m. the watchman raised the alarm that the floe was splitting. Our camp was reduced to an overcrowded rocking triangle, and it was evident that we must take the first opportunity to escape, no matter how desperate the chances might be."

At 8.00 the next morning – after almost losing one man in the water when the ice separated – Shackleton ordered the launching of the three ship's boats: the 22´ 6˝ whale boat *James Caird* was the sturdiest and most seaworthy; the *Stancombe Wills* and *Dudley Docker* were 21´ 9˝ cutters, designed for rowing, not sailing. As open boats they were not the equal of the severe seas they were to face.

Given their westerly position – and the fact that their only means of propulsion were oars and whatever small jury-rigged sails could be set up – it would be largely the ocean currents which would drive the boats forward. And Elephant Island was the only land ahead to which the sea might take them.

On 12 April, however, Shackleton realized that instead of running west, the little boats had drifted thirty miles east. Only Frank Wild, the second-in-command, and Worsley were told of this. But after this setback, tide and current were with them and the forbidding profile of Elephant Island was sighted to the north-northwest. On 14 April the men landed at the only place offering any sort of beach: a narrow strip of shingle – glimpsed through breaks in the foul weather – beneath the lowering 2000-foot-high cliffs of Cape Valentine.

The approach to Elephant had been fraught with dangers. A gale had separated Worsley commanding the *Dudley Docker* from the others during the night as they converged on the island, creating high and powerful seas which threatened to swamp them at every turn: frightening conditions to experience around an uncharted and rockbound coast in the dark, with the *Stancombe Wills* showing less than a foot of freeboard above the waterline. (Shackleton, in his book *South*, acknowledges his debt to Frank Wild, a tower of quiet confidence and strength, who sat at the tiller of the *James Caird* seemingly untouched by fatigue, "steel-grey" eyes scrutinizing the ice-filled ocean as calmly as if he was on a day trip in the Thames Estuary.)

The near-delirious joy of the men at being on solid land for the first time in sixteen months was moving to watch. But Shackleton knew the place could not be a long-term haven: with the beach a mere hundred feet wide and fifty feet deep, gale-swept high tides would bring the ocean to the very base of the cliffs. On the other hand, he did not know whether the island offered any other secure ground for camping. Next morning he despatched Frank Wild and four relatively fit men in the *Stancombe Wills* to search for a safer location. They returned in the dark having found a narrow spit of rock and sand seven miles to the west which appeared the only alternative "residential" site available.

The accounts left by both Shackleton and Frank Worsley of that seven-mile passage to Point Wild – as they were to name the constricted promontory Wild had discovered – through raging seas, are remarkable. They speak volumes for the seamanship, courage and leadership of Shackleton, Worsley, and Wild. Soaked to the skin, unsure of their destination, and in constant danger of being swamped or pushed against a lee shore of cliff and rock, they finally landed everybody on the narrow neck of land that was to be their home for 105 days. In fact, Worsley's boat was almost lost when he decided it would be safer to leave the lee of the cliffs and steer out to sea to round a rocky point, lest there be shoals on the inside route. Beyond the protection of the high cliffs, wind and sea nearly defeated him.

Shackleton, knowing there was no hope of rescue from Elephant Island, set off with five men in the *James Caird* – on Easter Monday, 24 April, at the start of the Antarctic winter – to try and reach a speck in the vastness of the South Atlantic known as South Georgia, lying 800 miles to the northeast. Frank Worsley went with the "boss", as Shackleton was generally called; Frank Wild was left in charge of the twenty-two men marooned on the island. With the benefit of hindsight, it seems likely that, without these two men, Shackleton's indomitable effort to save his company would have failed. It was Wild's gentle yet firm discipline, together with the example of his stoicism and serenity of spirit, that kept up the hopes of the slowly starving men in his charge. And it was Worsley's navigational skills, involving both dead reckoning and the handling of a sextant on a small boat buffeted by mountainous seas and gale-force winds – on those few occasions when a shot at the sun was possible – that finally got the *James Caird* close to South Georgia; yet it was a last-minute intuitive decision by Shackleton to change course slightly to the east that ensured that they did not disappear into the wastes of the South Atlantic.

Hurricane-force winds had driven the *James Caird* on to South Georgia's wild and dangerous southwest coast – a coastline which ships today still prefer to avoid: this meant that Shackleton had to attempt a seventeen-mile crossing of the island's alpine peaks, glaciers, and frozen lakes in order to reach help at Stromness whaling station on the east coast – a feat never before attempted. No one had ever penetrated more than one mile inland – and this only on the relatively benign east coast.

He set out on 15 May 1916 with Worsley and Tom Crean, second officer on the *Endurance*, leaving the sick men of the boat journey behind to await rescue. Thirty-six hours later Shackleton was in Stromness.

The achievement in making this first crossing of South Georgia in an Antarctic winter – immediately after the harrowing voyage of the *James Caird* – reveals the truly impressive power of Shackleton's will and courage, not to mention that of those men he selected to play vitally important roles in the survival operation. (Forty years later, in 1965, South Georgia was crossed again by the British Combined Services Expedition – hardened men

OPPOSITE: *Allardyce Range, South Georgia. "Shackleton had to attempt a seventeen-mile crossing of the island's alpine peaks, glaciers, and frozen lakes in order to reach help at Stromness whaling station on the east coast – a feat never before attempted."*

fitted-out with the latest and best equipment. They were under no pressures of time, could select their route carefully, yet found it treacherous and difficult going. Duncan Carse, the leader of the team, said that Shackleton, travelling at night, had perforce taken the most difficult route: "I do not know how they did it," he wrote, "except that they had to – three men of the heroic age of Antarctic exploration with fifty feet of rope between them – and a carpenter's adze."

The day after descending the mountains of the Allardyce Range into Stromness, Worsley was on his way back in a whaling steamer to pick up the three men left on South Georgia's southwest coast. And the day following Worsley's return to Stromness with the remainder of the *James Caird*'s crew, Shackleton, Worsley and Crean were heading for Elephant Island in the Norwegian whaler *Southern Sky*. This rescue attempt failed – as did two subsequent efforts: ice conditions and bad weather prevented any approach to the Island.

But on his fourth try – in a small steamer loaned by the Chilean government named the *Yelcho*, under the command of Captain Luis Pardo – a brief window in the weather allowed them to find a channel through the ice, and the ship was able to manoeuvre between icebergs and reefs, put a boat ashore, and take off the men who had lived for 105 days beneath the upturned *Dudley Docker* and *Stancombe Wills*. It was 30 August 1916. Thus, Shackleton became known as the leader who, when in command of an expedition, never lost a man in all his years on the ice.

Frank Worsley recounts how Shackleton, scanning the beach through binoculars, counted the black figures emerging from beneath the upturned boats; on reaching twenty-two he yelled to Worsley, "They're all there, skipper!" And when he lowered his binoculars it seemed to Worsley that the "boss" had shed years.

If Coleridge's *Ancient Mariner* had first engaged a boy's innate fascination for the legendary world of Antarctic ice, then our encounter with Elephant Island drove home the harsh reality of the region, helped one come of age, so to speak.

The historic spit of beach where the crew of Shackleton's *Endurance* sheltered now overflows with chinstraps. There is little room for humans to move around ashore without upsetting the colony. On the spit a bronze bust of Captain Pardo, Master of the *Yelcho* surveys the beach atop its high plinth – an incongruous, worldly touch in this remote and hostile place.

It is necessary to round the point in order to see fully the massive glacier behind the spit – the presence of which must have added considerably to the misery of the men of the *Endurance*. There are always rumblings of cracking ice sounding menacingly over the water, and substantial, loose portions of its rugged and serrated face – tons of fractured ice – constantly break away and fall into the sea, creating waves which can easily swamp a small boat or even a beach.

I try to imagine what it would be like to live on the pungent midden of a penguin rookery for almost four months through gale and blizzard, restricted to a low and narrow promontory surrounded by a restless sea, cliff and glacier at one's back allowing no temporary retreat from claustrophobia to a more spacious hinterland – a black-and-white world, utterly rock-bound and barren. I imagine myself walking up and down that slender saddle of shingle beach – day after day – the ocean sometimes crackling with piled floes and shards of ice, sometimes raging against the rocks to fill the air with freezing spray. I contemplate the long hours spent, day and night, plagued by frostbite and boils, lying jammed between one's companions in the blubbery soot-blackened atmosphere of an upturned boat – glaciers calving day and night with the percussive booms of a heavy artillery barrage as tons of ice slip into the sea; listening to the whine of the wind and beat of the swell. I wonder what those left behind were thinking the day Shackleton and his five crew left Elephant Island – knowing full well that if he did not get through they were all likely dead men. And then to be hit with a blizzard the very next day that lasted for two whole weeks. Worse: what it must have been like as, day by day, hope for Shackleton's return diminished.

The hunger came later when penguins left to winter in more northerly seas, and seals took to the water to forage beneath the sea ice and cut holes through which they would emerge to breathe and lie on its surface. One necessity for survival was, however, in ample supply: fresh water – always available in the form of glacier ice – a blessing when finally the group was reduced to boiling down kelp to make a thin and salty soup and digging through sand and shingle to recover the bones of seals, penguins, birds . . . to be boiled down to extract whatever slight nourishment they might provide. Time was fast running out when Shackleton finally returned. And through it all, stoical and fatalistic, the rock that was Frank Wild – encouraging, exhorting, announcing every morning as he rolled up his sleeping bag,

"Get your things ready, boys, the boss may come today." How marvellously he kept up the morale of those men when the chance of rescue was so remote – never could a leader's eyes have known such despair as he scanned the black and empty ocean every day.

Facing that massive glacier front, aware of the threat it poses, staring at the grim series of dogtoothed peaks guarding the island's interior, one feels a deep visceral emotion, a genuine empathy for the men who were stranded here. No book, no account or history can convey the brooding atmosphere of this place – it is only by standing where they stood, hearing, seeing and smelling their dark, constricted world, that one can even begin to identify with the men waiting, waiting on this strand. I have to ask myself the question: would I, in their position, have been up to it? My first response is, almost certainly not. Yet who knows what inner resources one might find when, as they say, "the chips are down"?

It is difficult to anticipate the strengths and weaknesses of the human spirit. It is as difficult to imagine withstanding the intense physical and psychological pressures experienced by the men of the *Endurance*. Yet each, to a man, from the charismatic leader to the most anonymous member of the crew, rose to the challenge and did what had to be done. One might argue that it is in the nature of the men who chose to do these things to fight for survival, not to break under pressure. Yet they were, after all, in so many respects, ordinary men – human beings who suffered grievously from hunger and cold, loneliness, and moments of utter despair.

Fearlessness, courage, resourcefulness, stamina – all are characteristics of almost any competent explorer. But Shackleton possessed two especially significant strengths, patience and faith, which elevated him to the status of a great one. He had patience in abundance – the will and ability to endure and sit things out until he intuitively knew the moment to act had arrived. And he exercised a most extraordinary faith in his own capabilities – a self-confidence which allowed him to triumph against what seemed to be overwhelming odds, and find a way out when all seemed lost. Not surprisingly, with this gift went a great ego – a dislike of being challenged or questioned and, at times, an inability to recognize or admit mistakes. At certain critical moments in the *Endurance* odyssey this inflexibility produced dissension, yet the majority of men under his command never lost their immense trust in his judgement, in his concern for them, and in his ability to get them home. When called upon to give of their best in dangerous situations, they did so, and followed "the boss" without reservation.

In his presence men felt the strength of Shackleton's spirit in all these particulars. A statement attributed to the Antarctic geologist Sir Raymond Priestley – in 1956 – sums up the capabilities of the leaders of the three major South Pole expeditions: he recommended Scott for scientific research; Amundsen for swiftness and efficiency in attaining his goal; but in the face of adversity, with no salvation in sight, then the answer was to get down on one's knees and pray for Shackleton.

I would add a footnote to this brief account of Shackleton's success in saving the men on Elephant Island. Both he and Frank Worsley, writing independently – and at different times – about their hazardous winter crossing of South Georgia's totally unknown glaciers and high peaks, tell of a strange phenomenon each experienced on the journey. You will remember there were three men in the mountain party – yet both Shackleton and Worsley speak of a fourth member: of sensing the presence from time to time of an invisible companion lending them support and guidance on this last and crucial leg of their incredible journey.

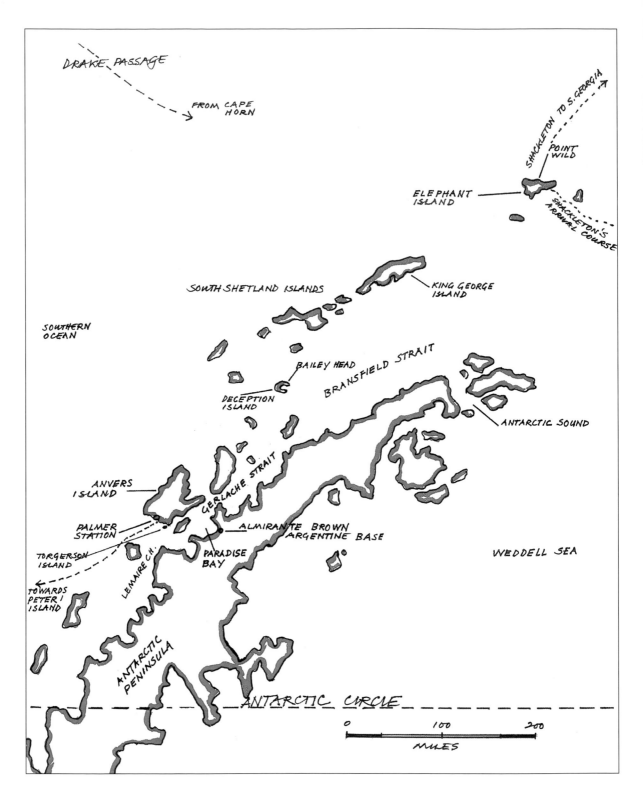

The Antarctic Peninsula and Islands

3

THE BEAUTIFUL AND THE FEARSOME

FROM THE ANTARCTIC PENINSULA TO PETER I ISLAND

After the South Shetlands . . . the Antarctic Peninsula: the 740-mile-long and mountain-spined finger of the continent reaching towards South America – access to which is gained by means of the spectacular waterway known as the Gerlache Strait. The Strait lies between the mainland of the Peninsula and a long chain of barrier islands separated by wide channels leading to the open sea. It is a narrow body of water regarded as the most

Gerlache Strait by day. "… the most evocatively beautiful – and certainly the most photographed – of all peninsula waterways."

evocatively beautiful – and certainly the most photographed – of all peninsula waterways: steep, Cyclopean slabs of black cliff on one side, vistas of sea and snow-covered mountain ranges on the other.

Yet the weather can be dramatic – snow flurries and small, fierce squalls rendering visibility almost non-existent. I have seen it under all conditions from storm to calm: the most splendid being when the water is mirror still, occasionally rippled by the gentlest of passing winds, and one has the strange impression of drifting aimlessly over some lost inland sea. And as the sun emerges from behind the clouds and shafts of light begin to play on the tops of the snow-covered cliffs before spreading into a glorious golden wash that flows all the way down to the surface of the water, there is created one of those supremely beautiful moments when the spirit can only exult.

Even in the Antarctic summer the air is cold and brisk. Down the middle of the channel small pods of minke whales surface and blow, feeding on clouds of krill and plankton, aware but unconcerned by anybody's presence. For as long as an hour or so they will feed, dive and play, their great bulks just visible beneath the dank, dark water,

The sun moves inexorably toward the horizon. Yet the Strait is too far north for it not to set, and soon it will disappear, albeit briefly. But in this exquisite moment of slowly fading light it is easy to imagine oneself present at the beginning of the world: there is no other place on earth, nor has there ever been. All of time and space are caught up in this place and this moment; we are, men and whales alike, ephemeral creatures of ice and water and light.

The Gerlache Strait leads into Paradise Bay. If dark and hostile Elephant Island saw the triumph of the human spirit, then Paradise Bay, though perfectly named when its pure snow and brilliant sunshine render it absolutely ethereal, is one place in the Antarctic where spirit failed. Here, at the head of the bay, stands a former Argentinean base known as Almirante Brown. Seen from a distance, it appears a welcoming cluster of barn-red buildings nestled against a clean white snowfield. As one approaches, however, it becomes apparent that the little base is abandoned and quite ruined. Many years ago, the story goes, the base doctor, overwhelmed by the prospect of wintering-over, suffered a severe

OPPOSITE: *Gerlache Strait at sunset. "… in this exquisite moment of slowly fading light it is easy to imagine oneself present at the beginning of the world."*

breakdown and set fire to the base. Why a man who had chosen to go there, who would be living at an hospitable base with at least basic creature comforts, and who could have been removed at almost any time, would snap so dramatically is a fascinating question. I suspect that, like the vast ice fields surrounding the base, his psyche was sabotaged with hidden cracks and fissures of which no one knew until it was too late.

A gentoo penguin rookery of several hundred breeding pairs is established on the northern side of the bay – together with a few chinstrap penguin couples who seem quite at home as a minority group. All penguin rookeries reek of guano – an acrid and nostril-piercing odour which would make a powerful decongestant agent – and the aroma at Paradise Bay is particularly malodorous, warning well in advance of the birds' presence. Most pairs have two chicks – well established – and I wonder if the nature and locality of the rookery has anything to do with this. The large, rounded rocks which comprise the breeding area offer both concealment and protection for the youngsters grouped around their bases – skuas must have a job both in selecting victims and pressing home an attack – while the waters of the channel, but a hop, skip, and jump away, provide easy feeding for the parents and thus shorter intervals between regurgitations for the chicks.

The gentoos are the loveliest of the penguins with their white eyebrows and bright red bills, and although they are closely related to the chinstraps they have a markedly gentler disposition. Curiosity and boldness are characteristic of chinstraps, but the gentoo is shy and will tend to retreat where the others will walk right up to you and look you in the eye. I walk slowly around the edge of the rookery trying not to intrude. It is Sunday morning and without having given it any previous thought I suddenly see in the gentoos before me a cloistered Catholic order, wimpled nuns serenely and devoutly going about their work. Then I remember the frenetic chinstraps on Deception Island, now seeming in contrast like evangelical activists, miniature Elmer Gantrys, rushing about, enthusiastically spreading the word of God. I think this morning I am more comfortable in the quiet company of nuns. The holy ladies ignore me as I take my seat beside them on the rock.

Pacem in terris – pacem in Paradiso.

The dramatic and geologically impressive cliff to the right of the ruined station is the breeding ground for a large colony of blue-eyed shags or cormorants. They gather like a sombre Greek chorus on the narrowest of

Birth of a gentoo chick. "The gentoos are the loveliest of the penguins with their white eyebrows and bright red bills …"

Cormorants at Paradise Bay. "They gather like a sombre Greek chorus on the narrowest of ledges, then slip one by one into the inky water …"

ledges, then slip one by one into the inky water and beneath the ice floes, diving deeply in pursuit of fish and squid. When they surface they stand on a rock with their wings outspread to dry, for unlike any other diving birds, they have no protective oil on their feathers. Standing motionless with their long necks and wings extended, they seem otherworldly, sinister even, their dark colouring appearing melancholy and almost threatening. But a wide ring of brilliant blue around the eye brightens the face and imparts an odd, even exotic, beauty to the head and gives an impression of a quick and penetrating intelligence. Returning to land, they face the cliff and leap onto the rocks, then walk with purpose to their messy nests, precarious affairs built of feathers, bits of seaweed and assorted rubbish and held together with guano and fresh droppings – a weak form of cement, able also to help anchor the nests to the rocks.

Dominating the bay, pulling the eye irresistibly from whatever local incidents are of interest, is the sea-going facade of its glacier. There is no escaping it. Even were it not visible – say in a whiteout blizzard – the sounds emanating from deep within its labyrinthine crevasses would prevail over all other perceptions: pistol-shot crackings, double-bass rumblings, the hiss and boom of calving ice hitting the water and causing the sea to boil and send out minor tidal waves.

This wall of ice stands about half a mile across the water from the derelict buildings of Almirante Brown, and runs east and west for roughly 400 yards. Set in such a mountainous context, and so jaggedly uneven at its rim, the height of its face is difficult to gauge – but I would guess it varies between 150 and 200 feet. Fissured, crumbling, greyed and dis-coloured over its rotting surface, blue-green in its cracks and holes, it lurks, giving the lie to the word "Paradise".

Bring together in the mind that black water, the floating small icebergs and chunks of brash, the surrounding high walls of dark rock crested with swags of sugar-snow, and crumbling cathedral-facades of ice – along with the sounding presence of the great glacier seemingly always at one's back – and you have a true and impressive microcosm of the Antarctic. If such is the case on a clear day with only a few low clouds clinging to the encircling heights, then imagine what it must be like with snow falling, wind whipping up small whitecaps, and glacier and precipice alternately appearing and disappearing in fleeting bouts of mist and cloud.

Drifting in such a raw, primordial world substantially diminishes the comfortable, self-important image one has built up over the years. I wonder if the legendary actions of the fire-setting doctor at Almirante Brown might not have resulted from such a total loss of identity when faced by a whole winter in Paradise Bay.

Lying due west of Paradise Bay, across the Gerlache Strait, is Anvers Island. Here a long, unbroken face of ice-cliff spills out into the sea as a continuation of the vast snowfield sweeping down from its high ground. It is more than half a mile long, made up of slabs of ice clearly defined by vertical cracks which run the full height of its face, a couple of hundred feet or more. The cliff face blinks on and off like a series of mirrors whenever the pale sun breaks free from the clouds and strikes the ice.

It is just after the sun disappears for a while, and the first flurries of

snow drift across the water in the half-light, that the sharp reports which herald the imminence of collapsing ice send shock waves into the air. There is a split-second silence. Then a deep *basso profundo* growl reverberates both beneath and within the ice, finally breaking free to become a series of cracking salvos sounding like multiple sonic booms. At the same time new and deeper perpendicular fractures appear across a hundred yard-long section at the centre of the ice wall.

The staccato explosions of fracturing ice sound ever closer together, and imperceptibly the whole central section of the ice cliff trembles uncontrollably as if it was but the flimsy backdrop to a stage set, a canvas surface rippling before a sudden squall. The sea swells and hisses as underwater ice becomes newly destabilized, and then the collapse begins.

With the tumbling of the first section – a huge buttress-like column capped by a jagged razor-edged pinnacle and perhaps forty feet by forty at the base – it is as if a salute of cannon commemorates the loss, a boom of sound that echoes and ricochets in the amphitheatre of the bay unable to escape heavenward, being dragged down by the tons of ice that slide slowly and painfully – tilting backward from the vertical – to their grave beneath the water. When the sea rushes back to fill the void thus created in itself, the rising spume forms an enormous fountain and the roar of the outward-thrusting wave sounds as a death knell. There is no pause: one massive ice block after another – sometimes two together – fracture, splitting from the parent cliff and sliding crazy-angled, and in slow-time, to the waiting sea. Those too large to be swamped ride high in the water, and float away as small icebergs on their own. And so it continues until the calving has created a small bay in the centre of the ice shelf. When it finishes – suddenly and unpredictably – the world is wrapped in silence. Even the sound of waves lapping against the shore is stilled.

How long did this avalanching endure? Difficult to say. Time becomes immeasurable when the senses are bombarded so intensely.

Torgerson Island is a forbidding, slightly domed islet of perhaps thirty black-rock acres, five minutes across the water from Anvers Island.

> OPPOSITE: *Anvers ice cliff.* "*... the whole central section of the ice-cliff trembles uncontrollably as if it was but the flimsy backdrop to a stage set, a canvas surface rippling before a sudden squall.*"

Today it is blustery and snowing. The island appears to be a small mountain fastness from which a number of icy peaks rise – an illusion created by the backdrop of grounded icebergs whose summits seem initially to spring from the rock itself. There are no giants among this ring of bergs – the highest point to be seen stands no more than sixty feet above the sea – yet they have been shaped by wind and ocean into striking architectural and sculptural forms: pinnacles and flying buttresses, sweeping curves leading the eye from point to point over rhythmically flowing concave and convex surfaces – a crystalline assembly of icing-sugar confections encrusted with a spidery tracery of frozen wind-whipped spray, and pierced with openings for cathedral windows that would have delighted Antonio Gaudí.

Devoid of penguins the place would be grim indeed. But the constantly shifting black and white kaleidoscope created by 15,000 pairs of breeding Adélies as they take their jerky little walkabouts, and the continual "whirr . . . whirr . . ." from thousands of penguin throats give life to the place, countering its barren and bleak appearance.

Penguins come in two sizes, large and small – a broad generalization, but true enough. Emperors and kings, standing an average height of three and a half feet, and colourful of plumage, are the larger birds. The smaller species comprise Adélies, chinstraps, gentoos, macaronis, rockhoppers: they stand about one and a half feet tall. Save for the macaronis and rockhoppers – with their yellow and orange crests – small penguins are totally black and white. Of all the penguins, only the emperor and the Adélie are considered to be true Antarctic specimens – that is to say, those who breed within the Antarctic Circle on or adjacent to the ice – but the Adélies are to be found everywhere: here in the northern Peninsula outside the Antarctic Circle, and as far south as Cape Royds in the Ross Sea, which is well within it. To many people, they are the most appealing of the penguins. Quick of movement, vivacious and intensely curious, they dash around with a sense of purpose and heroic indomitability.

A jumble of rocks leads steeply upward from the narrow beach toward the domed plateau of the island. At this first level, my attention is taken by a large crèche of well-advanced chicks guarded by only a few adult Adélies. This regiment of youngsters huddles closely together, well-drilled in keeping tight formation. If any chick strays beyond safe limits, one of the guardian birds hustles the offender unceremoniously back into the group, for predatory skuas are overflying the rookery, ready to pick off any adventurous stragglers, especially if they appear weak and undersized.

The crèche breaks up when parent birds – who have been at sea fishing – return to claim their offspring, freeing the senior guardians who are not breeding this season.

The snowfall is easing off; the wind is down. A narrow wedge of blue appears behind the backdrop of icebergs and air temperature has noticeably dropped. At a higher level, off to the left where a couple of skuas are wheeling low over a tall, triangular pointed rock, there is a flurry of activity. After a couple of circuits, each makes a shallow dive to skim the ground behind the protruding rock before returning leisurely to circle the target area. A certain number of skuas attach themselves to every rookery and fiercely protect it against other skua predators; for this service they exact payment in eggs and chicks – taking either the least well-protected or most infirm infants in the colony. Like all such selection in nature, this tends to strengthen the colony.

My presence does not affect a drama being played out in this corner of the rookery. I sit down a few yards away and watch. At the base of a sharp-pointed rock, huddled in a shallow hole, is an Adélie chick. It is doing its best to hide itself by pushing sideways into a cleft low on the stone. It is a sickly youngster, about fourteen inches tall, thin and stooped and moving with difficulty; its fluffy coat of down – not yet moulted to expose underlying sea-going feathers – is muddied and caked with patches of dried guano. There are no parents about. The bird has either wandered too far from the nest or been abandoned by the adults.

The skuas seem to be in no hurry – although I notice that as they circle the turns are becoming tighter, the dives less leisurely and taking a steeper angle. "Psychological warfare," I whisper to myself. "Intimidation."

The penguin has seen me. It has its head on one side, watching me out of the near eye. For a moment I contemplate trying to rescue the chick – to reach down and pick it up, place it in the centre of the colony where it would be surrounded by hundreds of others. But who would feed it? The youngster is certainly incapable of going to sea to fend for itself. Might he (she?) be adopted, find a foster parent? It is most unlikely, in which case the skuas would claim their victim even more easily as the chick weakened. Here at least the cleft in the rock is wide and deep enough to offer protection – and it might spare the young penguin the tearing and pecking death that flat ground would bring. The kill would be difficult for the skuas: they would have to work hard for their supper.

The beleaguered chick has dropped its head again. Its eyes are closed. Only the short stiff tail seems alive, juddering erratically from side to side every few seconds.

One of the skuas lands and begins to walk around the rim of the depression at the base of the rock, jumping casually over my feet. If the penguin sees its adversary's approach, it gives no sign. Head sunk low on its breast, the only movement comes now from its flippers – an almost imperceptible rise and fall, as though it were drawing breath through them like a fish through gills.

Swearing at the marauding skua, I jerk upright. The offender rises lazily, nonchalantly, into the air and rejoins its companion on the circuit. I bend down and touch the chick – cupping the back of its head in the palm of my hand. The membrane covering its eye slides upward; it stares straight ahead, making no attempt to move, save to raise its head slightly and gently press back against my hand. We stay like this for several minutes until I feel my limbs stiffening in the cold air, a cramp beginning in the muscles of both thighs. As I move, the youngster again turns an eye toward me, shakes its head slowly from side to side and stretches its neck. It seems to grow several inches. One of the skuas makes a low pass over the rock and pulls up in a steep climb to hover almost motionless in the air above the young bird. Down comes the chick's membrane shutter and the youngster shuffles blindly, uncertainly, as if unsure of its foothold. A thin stream of mucus drops from beneath its tail: a clear excretion – with no waste matter in it – no food has been taken for some time.

Minutes pass; the situation remains unchanged. The sickly bird appears to be sleeping. I feel impotent, helpless, and very sad that I can do nothing to help the weak bird at my feet which is now making another desperate effort to squeeze into the rock cleft. I feel unhappy – in a totally unsentimental way – that this creature will never know the sea as its element, never catch fish, never progress through the water by porpoising: flying through the air one minute to take breath, then diving beneath the surface of the water which is its true home.

I am uncertain about leaving: if I stay long enough the skuas may give up and go fishing on their own account. On the other hand, my presence may be intimidating the chick – preventing it from seizing an opportunity to head for the relative safety of the crowded rookery: given the chance, the youngster might still find the resources to escape.

"I'm going to walk up the hill and take a look at the others," I pronounce to the little penguin. "I'll be back in about ten minutes."

All is bustling activity on the rounded, stony summit. From this position the icebergs are in full view, grounded at various angles about 100 yards off the northern edge of the island. They are all the more impressive now as their flanks and contours are visible right down to the waterline. Long orderly lines of adult Adélies are queuing up, each bird patiently waiting its turn to enter the rock pools that lead to the sea and food. Equally long lines of returning penguins march purposefully back inland, replete with krill to regurgitate to their waiting chicks. Some parents within the rookery are still huddled over infants too young to be placed in the large guarded crèches: they keep a vigilant watch over their nests of small stones, constantly surveying the sky to monitor overflying skuas. Non-breeding adults in their second or third years, free of familial cares, strut about making beelines for unknown destinations, seemingly oblivious to the rest of the penguin world.

To my right two skuas are ripping apart a newly strayed chick – one at each end – beating their wings in the air to help give purchase and provide tugging power on the slippery guano-strewn rocks. And sounding above all this activity comes the rhythmic and steady "whirring" of the constant penguin liturgy.

Apprehensively, I retrace my steps down toward the shore in the direction of the sharp-pointed stone. The embattled young penguin has moved away from the rock's protective cleft and is standing in the middle of the hollow, looking up in my direction. One of the skuas balances teeteringly on the rim, its scimitar-like bill raised, wings fluttering as stabilizers. There is no sign of the second skua. But just as I am about to rush forward with a great waving of arms, the other predator comes in steeply over my head, levels out and, braking with feet advanced, wings spilling air, alights expertly on the apex of the stone.

Awkwardly, the little penguin turns away from the skua on the rim and faces the newcomer. A moment of absolute stillness as they confront each other. Slowly, the high-perched skua brings up its wings, curving them – tips straining to meet – to form a tall arch above its head . . . then it leans sharply and menacingly forward, head extended down toward the soiled and bedraggled prisoner in the hole, its beak opened wide to expose a gaping and soundless throat.

The small Adélie inches painfully toward its tormentor. Flippers extended for steadiness, it stops just short of the cleft in the stone, inclines its whole body toward the rapacious skua beak . . . and opens its mouth to be fed.

The Bellingshausen Sea is named after the Russian explorer, Thaddeus von Bellingshausen of the Imperial Russian Navy. It was during his remarkable circumnavigation of Antarctica between 1819 and 1821 that he discovered an obscure and isolated island which he named after Peter the First, Tsar of Russia.

Almost six hundred miles south of Anvers Island, Peter I Island is, in Antarctic lore, somewhat of a mystery. Even among the scientific community, there are few who have ever seen it, much less landed on it. The pack ice often extends twenty-five miles or more on every side. Even if there is no ice, the wind and sea, with swells up to forty feet, can break up a vessel like a matchbox. Only eight landings have been made since its discovery.

When we approach it, at eight o'clock, in the bright evening light of the Antarctic summer, the island appears as a small, dark smudge on the horizon. The seas are calm; the wind is slight. No ice in sight. Total silence grips the ship. Everyone from the captain to the most seasoned scientist seems to hold his breath as if the mirage might vanish if the island sensed our presence; or we might wake from what must surely be a dream.

We continue to draw closer and, still, there is no ice. But now one can see the great shards of icebergs which have been blown away from the island by a recent storm and are piled up in the west like the skyline of a small city. Apart from clumps of brash ice there is clear water all the way to the shore.

It is also the dramatic and awesome appearance of the land itself which keeps voices down, conversation practically non-existent. The eight-mile-long black rampart of unbroken cliff is forbidding – more intimidating and inhospitable than any landfall I have ever witnessed. These menacing bluffs of Peter I form a massive sky-reaching plinth supporting the almost centrally placed, 5750-foot-high volcanic peak. Streaks of thin red cirrus stream like pennants around the cone, lending a Valhalla-like aura reminiscent of the Norse Gods to the dark and brooding summit. I suppose it was just mythically inevitable that in 1929 the *Norvegia* expedition should have landed here and

Peter I Island. "… if there really is a God, He long ago abandoned this place, leaving it subject to the darkest, most violent forces of nature."
Drawing by Michael McCarthy after the original photograph
by Warren Krupshaw in the Scott Polar Institute

claimed the island for Norway, and that anchored off the barrier of gale-hurled ice lies a small ship of about 800 tons, flying the Norwegian flag and with a helicopter sitting astern: the M/S *Aurora*, transporting a Norwegian Polar Institute research team from Oslo.

The air is cold, the wind brings involuntary tears to my eyes. Despite my excitement and the prospect of setting foot on this virtually inaccessible island, I have a strange sense of psychological unease. I think to myself that if there really is a God, He long ago abandoned this place, leaving it subject to the darkest, most violent forces of nature. If time is measured here, it is in millennia, distance in light years. The two small, insignificant ships, hundreds of miles from land in any direction, even further from anything we might call human, could easily become little more than matchwood if the pack ice began to move.

It is difficult to explain the sense of isolation which comes from being so far from anything familiar – facing an environment so unforgivingly bleak and hostile. Everything here, the sheer cliffs and volcano in their blackness and redness, seem to be inimical to everything we have learned from Western civilization. Religion, music, art, science, gentleness, kindness, compassion – all are rendered meaningless in the face of this harsh and utter loneliness. Any philosophical heritage, scale of values, is abruptly thrown into question, shorn of any metaphysical certitude. In this context, all life must be accidental and purposeless, subject only to the laws of physics and biology, a manifestation of nature's capriciousness and cruelty.

A handful of us go ashore in a Zodiac multi-skinned rubber landing craft. It is the ninth recorded landing on Peter I Island.

Patricia and I walk down the beach. The soaring heights of black volcanic rock at the west end are totally exposed, thrown out like grand flying buttresses to meet the high cliff a hundred feet or more above the narrow strand. With feet sinking into fine black sand, I manage to progress to where the cliff face on the right curves like the arm of an immense amphitheatre into the ocean – a wall of rock composed of volcanic detritus fused together by intense heat, through which the sea has broken to form an arch fifty feet high or more. The water races between the rough, black walls, rising and singing as if exulting in its all-too-brief freedom from the imprisoning ice.

The strip of land is so hemmed in by cliff and buttress that it is necessary to retreat to the water's edge and crane one's head backward to take in the vertical scale of the precipice with its steep mantle of snow. High above the beach, the overhanging snow field – pitted and ice-sealed – balloons over the edge like the eaves of a steep-pitched roof. Even if it were possible to climb this razor-sharp rock, the way to the upper slopes would be effectively barred by this projecting swag of ice. As eyes adjust to such a vertical scrutiny of the heights, a flock of pure white southern fulmars sweeps over the edge of the cliff – peppering the black rock in concentrations so dense in places as to suggest patches of snow clinging to the upper ledges. They nest high on these crags, seemingly secure against the wild gales which batter the cliffs for days on end. In their swift, bright flight they seem no more substantial than thought, yet they are strong enough to withstand, with infinite grace, an environment perfectly capable of bringing me to my psychological knees.

We wander back along the beach, drawn to take a last look into the high vault of the arch. Eerie shadows mask the details of wall and column: the roof is in pitch-black space. The only light comes from the pale-red afterglow of a departed sun which, catching the flank of a small outer iceberg, is reflected to graze the surface of the ocean as it runs beneath the arch, bloodying that blackest of all water to suggest that here the sea gives access to the island's deep-seated volcanic core: to a fire-chamber that is merely dormant, not extinct.

I retrace my steps to the short stretch of open water between the floes. The grey-dark of the brief Antarctic night has finally settled over Peter I. Now bereft of even the faintest suggestion of warmth, the cindery black buttresses and cliffs, overhung by fields of snow and ice sweeping down from invisible heights, chill the heart: a Hades without the shades of the dead to render it even remotely hospitable.

"Be easier with a few respectable ghosts around," I say.

MacIntyre, the Zodiac driver, nods. "I know what you're talking about," he says. "You'd better be God the Father, Son, and Holy Ghost all by your blessed self if you intend staying around here for long."

We reverse slowly out into water littered with broken chunks of ice, then run northward parallel to the beach before heading out to sea to round the arch. The Zodiac rears sharply against the swell as we clear the awesome pillars of black tuff which, seen at sea level, seem to curve up and away into the dun night for hundreds of feet. The arch, seen from the water in this dim light, has the appearance of a grotesque mouth ravenously devouring anything brought to it on the black tongue of current. My unease returns.

An incandescent blue iceberg, about thirty feet high and gently domed, draws us like a beacon – ancient, venerable ice, formed over hundreds, perhaps thousands of years, and compressed until only the shortest wavelengths of visible light, the blues, can escape. We drift silently into the lee and rest against it. Two young Weddell seals are sleeping on a wide flange a few feet above the water. Awakening, they raise their heads, regard us without interest, then drop their heads and return to sleep. We remain motionless for what seems a very long time. Then a small Adélie approaches from around the backside of the ice. It has been fishing; a red stain of krill discolours its otherwise immaculate front. Putting its head to one side, it ambles to the stern and fixes the driver with a beady stare. It begins to peck at the pontoon, but, after a few minutes, it straightens up, shuts both eyes and begins to sway slowly from side to side as if falling asleep.

Neither of us speaks. Only the faint swish of rubber against the ice breaks the silence which has enveloped the iceberg and ourselves. Facing this luminous dreamscape of blue ice, the seals and penguins trustingly asleep within arm's reach, I feel myself being subtly drawn into the tableau until I am no longer a part of anything beyond the limits of this patch of ocean, this tiny blue realm of ice. Thoughts which just a little while ago I found so disturbing seem no longer relevant. There seems to be little reason to continue on, to go wherever it was we ought to be going. Even the veteran MacIntyre, with his eyes continuously watching the surface of the sea, seems reluctant to leave.

The long snaky-looking head of a leopard seal – rated with the killer whale in terms of predatory ferociousness – comes cruising through the water some thirty feet away on our starboard side.

"Shouldn't we scare him off?"

"Best leave it alone: they're unpredictable and can be bloody fierce. Been known to threaten Zodiacs."

"It's the penguin on the iceberg I'm thinking about."

"He's okay as long as he stays on the ice: a landed leopard seal's much less of a threat."

Then I see the tent – a small red tent, 1200 feet up, pitched close to the cliff edge, clinging precariously to the 20° slope of the snow field.

"Lads from the *Aurora*," says Macintyre. "Their helicopter took them up there. Researching something or other – first time they've been able to get near the place for years."

"They landed a helicopter that close to the edge? On that angle of slope? God, they could have just slipped off into the sea; or been blown off as they were coming in . . ." My voice trails off as I try to visualize the operation; the surgical delicacy of handling required; split-second reaction time to sudden wind eddies, downdrafts from the summit; the possibility of a whirring fall down the black face.

MacIntyre follows my gaze, the Zodiac wallowing in the slight swell, motor barely ticking over. "They don't actually *land* it – not on an ice slope like that. The pilot just keeps it hovering with the skids barely brushing the surface; the chopper remains airborne, just about, ready for a quick lift off. Still a risky business in this kind of terrain where the weather can change in minutes. How'd you like to sleep up there?" he adds with a grin.

"Can't imagine it." And indeed I can't. Awake every second listening for any change in the weather; not trusting oneself in sleep – all too easy to slip off the edge; and not forgetting that one still had to get down sometime, while the helicopter might not be able to get back up.

The wind has been steadily increasing and even in the lee of the blue iceberg we are beginning to bounce against it. Seals and penguins remain fast asleep. Small choppy waves are splashing against the gunnels, and as we move out from the protection of the ice, it is apparent that the small floes through which we approached the island several hours ago have been blown together to form a virtually unbroken barrier behind us. We are effectively cut off from the rest of the expedition and the ship.

MacIntyre surveys the ice situation in the lead before us. He pulls away from the blue "grotto" and slowly edges the Zodiac forward toward the high abutting headland with its buttressed arch. He shakes his head, but says nothing. The reason for his concern is soon obvious. Ice blocks fifty feet or so of the lead between a large grounded iceberg and the outside walls of the vaulted passageway. Where forty-five minutes earlier we were in open water – the seaway by which we left the beach – there is now a jam of ice floes.

There is only one option left to MacIntyre: the only way to bypass the obstruction is to ride the Zodiac *through* the tunnel and rejoin open water behind the ice barrier on emerging from the black-columned arches. My opinion on such a manoeuvre is not invited.

A quick burst of power pushes the Zodiac forward some seventy yards directly into the archway's maw; then a sharp swing of the tiller and we are facing the forbidding Gothic-ribbed underpass – about fifty feet out, dead centre, the Zodiac bucking what is now a heavy swell as the sea rises and falls against the cliff to our right. It is with some trepidation that I confront this cavernous black hole – a spectacular cleft when viewed head-on, framed by razor-sharp walls and pillars of jagged volcanic detritus rising forty feet to the apogee of the arch. And it is dark as hell – the slight curve of the tunnel's walls preventing one seeing completely through to the other end.

MacIntyre swings the bright beam of his heavy-duty flashlight over the water and deeply into the vaulted passageway: no underwater rocks or pinnacles breaking through. Yet although the passage seems free of such hazards, the light of the torch reveals two potential danger spots: a surging build-up of white water at the tunnel's entrance, and an extrusion of rock in the tunnel wall at the curve that obviously narrows the passage.

"Hold the light," says MacIntyre, playing the throttle, feeling the drift in the constantly moving sea, summing up the situation at the tunnel's spiked and vertically thrusting mouth. Obviously what was but a slight freshening of the weather out beyond the island is intensified here where offshore wind collides with the eddies funnelling down from the heights to form capricious inshore gusts; where the sea – swelling into the tunnel from our corner of the headland meets the water flowing through from the other side – and forms a standing wave: a barrier alternating in height between two and three feet, rearing stiffly against any small boat planning entry.

He turns the Zodiac away; makes a couple of wide circles. There is only one way to take a rubber boat against a wave like that – especially when operating in such a restricted space – and that is to try and breach it as the water ebbs away from the base, and before it flows back to restore the wave to maximum height. This is best done by slithering over the crest at a slight angle, applying just enough power to climb up and over, then releasing the revs in order to slide down the other side and so maintain directional control over forward momentum.

MacIntyre goes round a third time – deciding the angle and speed of attack; noting the pattern of ebb and flow at the entrance; determining how to negotiate the turn where the tunnel narrows. "Move to the left side – closer to the stern – get your left arm around that security rope. Keep that light up now – beam dead-centre – low enough to show the lower walls and top of the water. Okay?" MacIntyre doesn't look anxious: just gives a sort of silly half-grin.

He opens the throttle. The Zodiac surges forward, bow just out of the water, approaching the buttressed archway from the left. A gusting downdraft pushes the nose to the right. A quick burst of power, touch of left rudder, brings it round again. Turbulence beneath the boat – like running over rows of cobblestones. The wave stands just forward of the entrance. MacIntyre is playing the throttle in short bursts – approaching like a boxer making swift thrusting jabs at an opponent, edging in, waiting for the right moment to slide up and over the obstructing crest. He eases off on the engine – lets the following sea push the boat forward – keeps just sufficient throttle to maintain headway until the bow is lifting steeply on the upswell and then, with a blip of the outboard, he powers the stern over the barrier-wave. At once it is necessary to counter the strong flow of water coming against the Zodiac from the opposite end of the underpass and pushing us close, far too close, toward the outside row of black lava columns supporting the vault: jagged, point-encrusted rock that could shred rubber like paper should the boat be driven with any force against it.

He inches the Zodiac forward against the current: a constant struggle of throttle and rudder against crosscurrents in a passageway no more than twenty feet wide.

I play the beam of the torch over the surface of the water, illuminating both the scabrous face of the headland-cliff on the right and the elephantine bulges of the sea-washed pillars to the left. The light does little to relieve the Stygian volcanic gloom – simply picks out the sea's motion and the lower levels of the passageway – the bends and narrowings of the tunnel.

With the first tricky turn and turbulent water behind us, the sky to the east is now completely visible beneath a much wider arch than that we faced at the western entrance. We go roaring through the final stretch and into the open lead running alongside the black sand beach.

MacIntyre is grinning all over his face. "Well, there's no going back that way. Have to thread up these short leads ahead of us. Hope there's water all the way. Might take us all night to find a way through!"

But the sky is already growing lighter. The sun is returning. High on the crags the fulmars swoop and shimmer like fireflies on a warm summer night.

4

LITTLE ICE, BIG ICE

THE ROSS ICE SHELF, ROSS ISLAND, AND SHACKLETON'S
DASH FOR THE POLE

The Bellingshausen Sea is behind us; the greater part of the Amundsen Sea is
already crossed; the Ross Sea lies ahead on a more southerly course. We are
encountering the first sea ice, not a solid pack, but brash ice, broken pieces of
the pack generally less than six feet across, around which large patches of
brownish plankton appear as discoloured areas on the surface of the sea, as
well as frequently showing as a crust on the underside of the ice. Plankton is a
rich source of food for sea birds – so much so that an ornithologist once
estimated that in a plankton-rich area such as this a single iceberg supported a
population of more than two thousand Antarctic petrels.

Sailing roughly in the latitude of 70° south and following the coastline
of West Antarctica at a safe distance beyond the edge of pack or fast ice,

we are, nevertheless, made aware of the ice presence by frequent iceblinks on the horizon – flashes in the sky occasioned by the reflection of a large body of ice close to the horizon. It was Captain James Clark Ross of the Royal Navy who sailed this sea and gave it his name. Between 1840 and 1843 he made three voyages in his two barque-rigged, ice-strengthened ships, the *Erebus* and the *Terror*. Sailing from Hobart, Tasmania, he first discovered Cape Adare at 71° south, then continued south to enter and name McMurdo Sound before turning east to confront and travel the length of the now famous Ross Ice Shelf – the floating body of ice known as the Barrier which is fed by the great glaciers of the hinterland, and which is roughly the size of France.

We are already nine days out from Peter I, but towards the end of the following day a vast, unbroken line of white cliffs, throwing off a radiant sheen into the sky, begins slowly to materialize in the southwest. The air is so clear that, even so far away, the blink from this enormous mass of floating ice is brilliant – for light is striking the surface of ice 1000 feet deep and refracting back into the sky, its brightness intensified, almost incandescent. At last we have reached the legendary 200-foot-high cliffs of the Barrier – a rampart of ice extending in length for over 400 miles.

As one draws nearer, this powerful iceblink gradually and subtly changes colour. Almost imperceptibly, the reflected light forms into bands of rose and gold above the sheer white of the ice shelf. The eye is led in over the dark blue surface of the ocean, deflected skyward by a vertical cliff face of pristine whiteness to the delicate rainbow hues of the upper air.

Imagine such a sight witnessed for the first time by the crew of Ross's 1841 expedition. On board the *Erebus*, James Savage, armourer and blacksmith, dictated his impressions to C. J. Sullivan, a mess-mate:

> On the morning of the Eight D° [February 1841] we found our Selves Enclosed in a beautiful bay of the barrier. All hands when the[y] Came on Deck to view this the most rare and magnificent Sight that Ever the human Eye witness[d] Since the world was created actually Stood Motionless for Several Seconds before he Could Speak to the next man to him.

OPPOSITE: *Ross Ice Barrier. "… the blink from this enormous mass of floating ice is brilliant – for light is striking the surface of ice 1000 feet deep …"* Photo: Colin Monteath

57

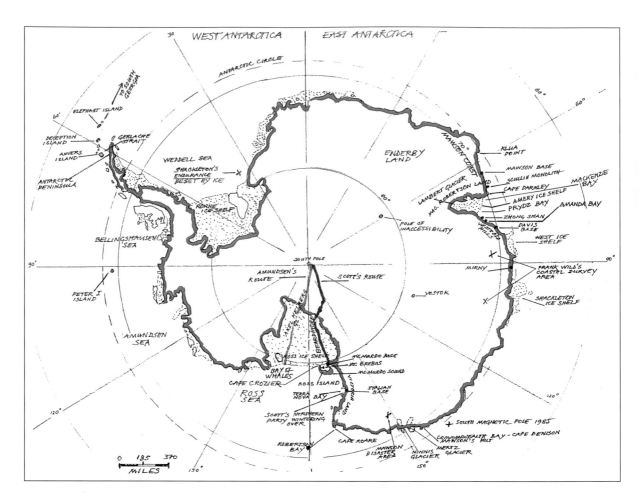

Places around the Antarctic continent mentioned in the text

Beholding with Silent Surprize the great and wonderful works of nature in this position we had an opportunity to discern the barrier in its Splendid position. Then i wish[d] i was an artist or a draughtsman instead of a blacksmith and Armourer We Set a Side all thought of mount Erebus and Victoria's Land to bear in mind the more Immaginative thoughts of this rare Phenomena that was lost to human view

In Gone by Ages

When Cap[tn] Ross Came on deck he was Equally Surpriz[d] to See the Beautiful Sight Though being in the north Arctic Regions one half his life he never see any ice in Arctic Seas to be compar[d] to the Barrier.

This is no mere facade of a large glacier, but the coastline of a "country" of solid ice. The ice shelf itself is on the move, flowing northward from the

58

land to the Ross Sea at the rate of about one mile a year. The glaciers which feed it – to landward on the continent proper – are huge in their own right, the most distant being the Reedy Glacier some 490 miles to the southeast. Add to the glacial feeding the accumulation of snow on its upper surface and one can appreciate how this spectacular shelf represents a giant, sea-going extension of the continental ice sheet, the cap which covers about 95 per cent of the land of Antarctica.

There are several such ice shelves, burgeoning from the glacier complexes of both West and East Antarctica, and they are estimated to form one third of the total Antarctic coastline. The huge tabular icebergs – some more than 200 square kilometres in area – found drifting in the high latitudes of the Southern Ocean, propelled by currents and wind, originate from such ice shelves: they are large sections which have broken away, or calved, from the leading edge of a main body such as "the Ross".

The Barrier is in many ways the symbol of the Heroic Age of Antarctic exploration. In order to reach the high plateau giving access to the South Pole, one had initially to cross this immense blizzard-swept, crevasse-ridden obstacle. First came Scott on his 1902–03 *Discovery* expedition, who turned back after slogging over 300 miles without being able to ascend to the Polar Plateau. Then, Shackleton on the 1908 *Nimrod* expedition sledged the full 400-mile width of the Barrier to discover the Beardmore Glacier and climb its 125-mile length to the Plateau, only eventually to turn back from the South Pole when just 97 nautical miles away.

In 1911, Roald Amundsen established his base camp at the eastern end of the ice shelf at the Bay of Whales – gambling that the ice on which the base was built would not break away into the Ross Sea before he returned –as he did in January 1912 after a faultlessly executed dash to the Pole. In March of the same year, Robert Falcon Scott and the rest of his Polar party, after discovering that Amundsen had reached the Pole before them, perished on the Barrier on their return. Their ill-fated journey was an incredible saga of physical suffering endured to the end through great strength of will and spirit. Unfortunately, all the will in the world could not withstand the blizzards and extreme cold of the Barrier in that autumn of 1912.

Both Scott and Shackleton began their own heroic journeys from Ross Island, at the far western edge of the Barrier. This island was discovered by Ross at the end of January 1841 on the first of his historic three Antarctic voyages. Ross had already been first to the north magnetic pole in the Arctic and was now embarked on a search for the south magnetic pole to make corresponding measurements.* Unfortunately, he was bound to be frustrated in this endeavour as the pole lay inland beyond the Victoria Land mountains. (Today it's located at sea off the Terre Adélie coast.)

Ross Island is a huge rock outcrop in a world of ice, linked to the Barrier along its southern side. Its western flanks abutting McMurdo Sound are also icebound for much of the year. Ross Island could equally well be called Volcano Island, for it was the fusion or coalescence of three volcanoes – Mounts Bird, Erebus, and Terror – which formed the land we see today. Only Mount Erebus, at 12,400 feet above sea level, is currently active.

The run of history has ensured that Ross Island should become one of the best known sites in the Antarctic. Captain Ross named two of its volcanoes, Erebus and Terror, after his ships; the third, Mount Bird, he named after Lieutenant Bird, first officer of *Erebus*, who had been with him in the Arctic. Cape Crozier, with its near-inaccessible emperor penguin rookery, bears the name of Commander Crozier, Ross's longtime friend and captain of *Terror*.

Alas, subsequent events were not kind to either of the two stout vessels which had served Ross so well in the Antarctic – nor to the redoubtable Commander Crozier. In 1848 both *Erebus* and *Terror* and their commanders – the now Captain Crozier, and Sir John Franklin, the expedition leader – were lost with all their men off King William Land in the Arctic attempting to find the elusive and tortuous Northwest Passage.

The grand spread of sky and land is welcome after the steep mountains of the Peninsula, where space and light is often claustrophobically trapped. Now, as we round Ross Island's northern shore and turn south into the wide open water of McMurdo Sound the horizontal expansiveness of the panorama is breathtaking. These limitless vistas and aerial perspectives belong to the Antarctica of history and popular imagination: mile upon mile of shimmering white snow and ice glistening beneath a vast sky – a sky capable of generating the most powerful of winds, the most

* The north and south geographic poles are the fixed axes around which the earth spins. The magnetic poles on the other hand represent the shifting axes of the earth's northern and southern magnetic fields which, basically, move according to the changing electrical conductivity of the earth's upper mantle.

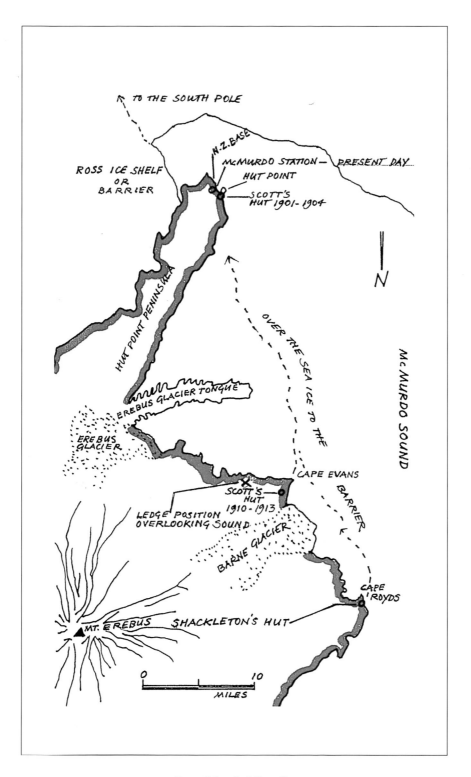

Ross Island: West Coast

impenetrable of blizzards or drifts; it is a huge land in which long journeys with sleds and dogs became odysseys, the kind of polar travelling which demanded the utmost in courage and endurance.

The coast on our left is still besieged by small, grounded icebergs. No beaches. Just outcropping large rocks defining the shoreline. Beyond the coast the terrain slopes gently upward in a series of small escarpments – a patchwork quilt of black exposed rock and stretches of virgin snow to the massive bulk of Mount Erebus, a wide-based symmetrical cone commanding the Sound, visually dominant, a plume of volcanic steam rising lazily from its crater. My first impressions are of the mountain's enormous girth and the seemingly limitless lateral spread of its sloping snowfield. But it also provides my first experience of the illusory nature of visual perceptions in the wide-open vastness of white Antarctica – for the volcano's snow-covered slopes appear deceptively accessible, almost close enough to reach after a short walk, seemingly right on one's doorstep.

Further south along the western shore of Ross Island is Cape Royds, a relatively unprotected bluff, named after Lieutenant Charles Rawson Royds, first lieutenant of the *Discovery* during Scott's 1902–03 expedition. It was here, in some desperation after finding his first two choices of a base location inaccessible, that Ernest Shackleton erected the *Nimrod* expedition's hut in January 1908.

Once ashore, I find Shackleton's hut situated in a hollow lying between the ridges and slopes of the region's many small hills, with the furthest south Adélie rookery to the seaward side and Mount Erebus dominating the hinterland. The building's dimensions of 33 × 20 feet seem hardly adequate to house fifteen men: in this small space they had to eat, work, sleep, worry, and meet all other social commitments. Only Shackleton had his own cubicle.

The hut's simple furnishings – pots, pans, and other items of equipment – remain in place roughly where they were left when *Nimrod* took everybody back to England in 1909. A picture of King Edward VII – the monarch who, liking Shackleton's style, knighted him on his return – hangs on the wall. Tins of food not used by the 1908 expedition are stacked against one of the outer walls, their labels (and possibly their contents) still well preserved – beef stew, lentils, etc. – testifying to both the refrigerator-like cold and the continent's almost desert-like dryness.

I try to imagine living in the place through an Antarctic winter; note the

Shackleton's hut – exterior. "Once ashore, I find Shackleton's hut is situated in a hollow lying between the ridges and slopes of the region's many small hills, with the furthest south Adélie rookery to the seaward side …" Photo: Colin Monteath

impressive size of the stove, a definite plus, the cramped sleeping arrangements, the dark and narrow entrance way which functions as a primitive freezer. Once again I am acutely aware of the total sense of isolation the men here must have experienced in 1908, knowing that no other human beings resided on this vast continent and that the nearest inhabited land was 2500 miles away. They knew that for much of the year the sea ice would cut them off from any contact with home and loved ones – and prevent their own departure by ship should an emergency arise – and that the long winter days of almost total darkness might bring psychological burdens far more serious than the physical ones.

As I leave the hut, I am greeted by the pleasing cadences of "whirr, whirr . . ." emanating from thousands of Adélie throats. Standing for a while, I watch the scurrying antics of the birds before skirting the rookery to climb the rocky rise to the shoreline. It is a good position from which to look back and see the hut in its context, close to a small ice-ringed lake and surrounded by ledges and hillocks, Erebus looming in the rear. With the amphitheatre-like sweep of the rookery sheltering it from the winds of ocean, the site possesses an intimacy not unlike that offered by a wild and rocky natural "garden" – a snug and almost cosy domesticity – not a common characteristic of Antarctic hut sites.

On turning round to face the ocean again I see a cluster of young adult Adélies gathered on the round nub of a rock column which stands about fifteen feet above the water. They stand stiffly erect, shoulder to shoulder, flippers down by their sides, like raw recruits on a parade ground. If one sways slightly, all the rest are set in motion. It is late in the season and the life of the rookery is winding down: these youngsters – newly rejected by their parents, or so I suspect – now have to fend for themselves, to go to sea for their own fish. So here they are, leaving home for the first time to make their own living, black-and-white-and-clean-as-a-whistle in their new sea-feathered suits, looking nervously on the vast strange world of ocean, waiting for somebody to make the first move.

And someone finally does. A penguin standing precariously on the edge of the rock pinnacle, distinguishable because it has been staring head-down at the water, suddenly draws itself up and dives. Instinct has triumphed: for the first time in its life the bird swims, heading for an ice floe some yards offshore, hurling itself through water and air in an impressive series of leaps which transform an awkward landlubber of a bird into a streamlined aquatic meteor. The rest look on, expectant, rippling in a collective movement to look down on the water.

And then, out of the ocean, midway between land and floe, surfacing at the aggressive angle of a marauding submarine, crashes the sleek profile of a leopard seal.

For a brief moment I am held in a state of suspended animation together with the Adélies on their column – they stand transfixed, frozen in a common shock of awareness. I doubt if any of us drew breath in that second or so of shock.

The leopard seal lunges forward to intercept the venturesome penguin as it leaps from the water, and takes the bird in the air, pinning it between the needle-like teeth of its powerful jaw – holds it there briefly, then bites down and breaks the young penguin's neck. The sharp, sickening crack is clearly audible in the dry air – like a branch snapping from a tree in winter frost. With two or three quick flicks of its head the seal shakes the penguin from side to side. When the body falls to the water it is not in one piece. In

64

Adélie penguins and leopard seal. "Heads turn frenetically this way and that, eyes looking past those of their companions into some vague but danger-filled distance."
Photo: Colin Monteath

the blink of an unbelieving eye the skin has gone in one direction, the flayed red carcass in another.

Every bird on the rock platform is moving restlessly, twisting from side to side, back and forth, their untested sea-feathers rustling – bird against bird – like the dying breath of an offshore breeze. Heads turn frenetically this way and that, eyes looking past those of their companions into some vague but danger-filled distance.

What happens next takes me totally by surprise. As if on command, all movement among the birds has abruptly stopped. For about three or four seconds every penguin is quite still, head cocked very slightly to one side in an attitude of concentrated attention. Then, as one, they take to the water in a perfectly regimented shallow dive. All the way out to the ice floe they seem to be flying in tight formation rather than swimming.

At this the leopard seal begins to dart and thrash about on the surface in seeming indecision, unable to select and home-in on any one victim – disoriented, I think, by the glistening flight of so many aerial projectiles.

The water in the vicinity is churned to a froth by the speed and force of the penguins' eruptions from it, the air shimmering with thousands of droplets of spray. The operation is all over in about ten seconds: the air clears and the sea settles down. Every fledgeling – save the first sacrificial victim – has made it safely to the ice floe. The leopard seal disappears beneath the surface of the sea.

Leopard seals do not confine their attacks to smaller creatures such as penguins. During those long months on the ice the men of Shackleton's *Endurance* expedition experienced the ferocity of the leopard seal at first hand.

One attack was not without its humour. Seal or penguin meat was often not available for long periods, and on occasions when supplies were running low leopard seals were the most readily available source of sustenance. The story is told of a leopard seal sighting when the shortest member of the party was deployed to the edge of the ice. There he stood, flapping his arms about to imitate a penguin in the expectation that the seal would attack and could then be shot. But the animal's assault across the ice was so fast and aggressive that all were thrown into disarray, and no one more than the unfortunate decoy.

On another occasion, Orde-Lees – the one generally responsible for husbanding all supplies – returning from a hunting foray and travelling on skis across suspect, melting sea ice had almost reached the encampment when the malignant, snake-like head of a leopard seal came crashing from the sea just in front of him. He immediately turned and ran, thrusting hard with his ski poles and yelling for Frank Wild to get his rifle – Wild being the acknowledged sharpshooter of the party. In the meantime, the creature leapt from the water after Orde-Lees and with a few bounds was almost upon him. Then it veered off the ice and again took to the water. At this point Orde-Lees had almost reached the opposite side of the ice floe and was about to jump cross to stable ice when the sea leopard's head erupted from the sea right in front of him. The animal had, underwater, pursued his shadow across the rotten ice. As it lunged at Orde-Lees its enormous armoury of sharp-pointed teeth caused the man's calls for help to become screams as he turned and attempted to get away from his attacker.

Again the predator sprang from the water to the ice in pursuit of Orde-Lees at the moment when Wild appeared with his rifle. Catching sight of

Wild, ferocity undiminished, the leopard seal then turned to attack him. And although Wild fired repeatedly at the on-rushing creature, the momentum of its charge was such that it was less than thirty feet away when it finally dropped to the ice.

I decide to take a short cut by walking alongside the lake instead of following the higher ground around it. That this brings Patricia and me into the heart of a skua nesting area is not something to which I have given much thought until, suddenly, there are four or five of them wheeling above my head. A half-dozen more appear on the higher rocks around me, standing with their wings unfurled and swept upwards like Gothic arches – their ravening beaks open to the throat in soundless defiance: they are so eagle-like that it is difficult to link them with the gull family from which they have evolved. Certainly the transformation that occurs when a skua ceases to sit quietly, looking like a brownish oversized pigeon, and takes to the air, or stands tall in menacing display, is remarkable.

I have been at close quarters with skuas before, but always within a penguin rookery – such as the occasion on Torgerson Island with the besieged Adélie chick. In that context they take little notice of one – their own chicks are not threatened; they are too busy hunting or defending "their" rookery from other predators themselves. Now, because I have not paid enough attention, we are in the middle of their territory, a potential threat to their nests and young.

I stop walking for a moment: an image from the past is struggling to take shape – the Stuka the German dive-bomber of the Second World War that came down on one screaming in a 90° vertical dive – perhaps, for me, the most chilling sound of the war. It was not just the scream, but the aircraft's ability to point its nose at the ground and dive almost vertically on to the target in a precision attack, guns hammering, before releasing its bombs, that made it the most feared weapon in the German arsenal for those on the ground.

As the skuas circle menacingly overhead, I note the dive-bomber silhouette, aware at the same time of their ability to come down steeply on a ground target and pull out at the last moment after driving home an attack. Then, warily watching the birds on the rocks, I am struck by how closely their physique matches the aeronautical design of the Stuka: solid and immensely strong across the shoulders or centre-section to withstand the stress of high speed descent; an impressive breadth to the wings where they join the body or fuselage; broad and flexible tails together with pronounced trailing-edges to the wings acting as highly effective elevators and air-brakes; a high dihedral angle from the root of each wing to the shoulder which facilitates the spill of air in the dive. These are all design elements which permit the steepest of descents, highly effective braking, and a quick recovery of altitude. Noting their aggressive stance, I remember cowering in a ditch on an airfield in southern England in 1940, absolutely convinced that the oncoming Stuka had me personally in its sights.

'Skua, skua, skua . . . Stuka, Stuka, Stuka . . ." The jingle sounds over and over in my head. More than just an alliterative catchiness of words, it is a significant linking of two events – the Stuka of nearly half-a-century ago, and the imminent threat from the Cape Royds skuas right now.

The attack comes very quickly. Without warning, the skuas on the rocks take to the air like a squadron of fighter pilots to join the four already aloft. Then down they come. I raise my arm high, believing, as I have been told, that the skua will attack the highest point of the target. These birds obviously know nothing of the theory. They come directly for my head. Gathering speed in the dive, they attack from every direction – back, front, and from the side – first levelling out to just brush my cheek or the back of my neck, and then returning to actually strike with the hardened edge of the wing. The attack is so orchestrated that I have to look around to see from where the next sortie might come. I manage to gain some protection by jumping around and waving both arms, yelling profanities, but there is always a bird which comes in on the blind side. Receiving a particularly sharp blow to the forehead I decide to run for it. If I can get beyond the nesting area, the skuas will, perhaps, abandon the assault. However, the onslaught increases as if the birds are infuriated by my attempt to escape. Partially blinded by the beating wings, stumbling on the uneven ground, I am brought to my knees, hands raised to protect my head – and the birds are coming from every direction.

I suddenly realize I am behaving as a victim – sinking ever lower and lower beneath the fury of their attacks – and in a spasm of rage push up to regain my feet and begin to lash out at them once again. The birds, perhaps momentarily startled, hold off slightly, and I walk rapidly away, resisting the temptation to run.

The skuas continue to circle closely, following me threateningly, then, as

Skua attack. "Gathering speed in the dive, they attack from every direction – back, front, and from the side – first levelling out to just brush my cheek or the back of my neck, and then returning to actually strike with the hardened edge of the wing."

abruptly as it had begun, the attack is over and we continue unmolested to the edge of the nesting area. When I look back, they are once again sitting peacefully on their rocks as if nothing had ever happened.

I am reminded of the the account by Carsten Borchgrevink of his expedition to Cape Adare in 1899 – the first group ever to winter-over in Antarctica and witness the spring return of penguins and skuas: "We daily saw fresh proof of the audacity of the skua gulls. On several occasions they attacked the dogs, and nearly all of us were attacked by them on more than one occasion. They shot down from a great height in the air straight onto our heads, hit us with their wings, only to rise again and renew the attack."

An air of tranquillity overspreads Cape Royds in the late evening when I return. The light is overall pearl-grey with a gleam of coppery orange bleeding in from around the horizon. The water is like glass. Ice free. Not a scrap of wind. I wonder if Shackleton had ever known it to be like this, in an Antarctic summer. A walk of fifty yards through a cleft in the shoreline bluffs brings me out on the southern flank of the Adélie rookery; the west-facing side of the hut lies immediately ahead. The light plays strange tricks with Erebus, pushing it further into the middle distance than I remember it from the afternoon, and blending the snows of the smoking summit to match the tones of the surrounding sky.

The rookery is unusually quiet; the cadences of soft Adélie chanting, rising first from one side then the other, suggest a liturgical ritual such as vespers or evensong – enhancing the sense of timelessness which suffuses the place this night. The birds are moving around as always, but their comings and goings are muffled and low-key, as if they themselves are responding to the mood of evening, or are aware that the colony is coming to the end of its existence for the year. Parents now refuse to feed their voracious offspring, and are being followed everywhere by chicks expecting the adult mouth to open and food to be disgorged. But the older birds know that summer is on the wane and that they must all leave soon for the north, to the edge of the pack ice and beyond if they are to fish and survive throughout the coming autumn and winter. To this end, the youngsters must be forced, through hunger, to go fishing for themselves. Meanwhile, the patrolling skuas fly in a desultory way: there is not likely to be much for them on the ground, anyway – no eggs, no small and manageable chicks for the taking. The skuas, too, must soon resort to their pelagic ways and become fishermen. In another few weeks Cape Royds will be devoid of living creatures: only the remains of late-born chicks who had not had time to moult and gain their sea-feathers will testify to the rookery's recent occupation.

Standing alone in a corner of Shackleton's hut by the narrow entrance corridor, I am affected by an atmosphere quite unlike that experienced during the afternoon when the hut seemed to be simply a memorial to an epic event in Antarctic history.

The men of Shackleton's *Nimrod* expedition, who lived here for so many months, accomplished nearly everything they had set out to do. Six of them – including Douglas Mawson who was later to become celebrated as an Antarctic explorer in his own right – made the first successful ascent of Mount Erebus. Mawson measured the crater and found it to be 900 feet deep and 2640 feet across. None of the party was a mountaineer and the climb exhausted them; so, knowing that time was of the essence, they made a rapid but risky descent by sliding down the side of the mountain.

When Shackleton set out with his companions for the South Pole, a separate three-man party took sledges north into the horrific terrain and weather of Victoria Land to ascertain the region of the wandering south magnetic pole. Two Australians, Professor Edgeworth David and Douglas Mawson, together with Alistair Mackay, an English naval surgeon, made up this group and accomplished their task; yet in doing so, found the threat of sudden death to be their constant companion in the form of the terrible crevasses down which one or another would regularly disappear, together with constant hunger, frostbite, and such severe cold that the skin was stripped from their lips. (Mawson woke every morning unable to open a mouth glued shut with congealed blood.)

Shackleton meanwhile, accompanied by Frank Wild, Eric Marshall, and Jameson Adams, almost became the first expedition leader to stand at the South Pole. After a terrifying journey up the crevasse-ridden, 125-mile-long Beardmore Glacier which rises over 6000 feet to provide access to the Antarctic Plateau (itself lying at an altitude of 10,000 feet), Shackleton turned back when just ninety-seven nautical miles from the Pole. The weather had treated them cruelly – headwinds cut them to the bone – and they were weak from lack of food: very close to starvation. Shackleton and Wild only just made it back to the Barrier, leaving Marshall, suffering badly from dysentery, some forty miles behind them, on the ice shelf in the company of Adams who was to look after him. *Nimrod* had picked up the magnetic pole party and planned to leave on 26 February, hardly expecting to see Shackleton or his group again. Shackleton and Wild reached the coast on 28 February. They saw no sign of the ship which was sheltering alongside a nearby glacier tongue – still waiting – and set fire to a small hut on the southern tip of Ross Island. The *Nimrod* men saw the flames and the two returned explorers were soon on board. Three hours later Shackleton was off leading the rescue party to recover Marshall and Adams. But I think it should be said – without prejudice to Shackleton's own courage and leadership – that were it not for the coolness and unflagging perseverance of Frank Wild in moments of crisis, and the example of his unfailing calm and workmanlike attitude to the job in hand, the group might not have found the resources to persist in the face of the adversities which beset them.

They had walked for 128 days of blizzard after blizzard, through deep soft snow and over razor-sharp ice, ascending and and descending the long

Beardmore Glacier, to cover a total of 1700 miles and achieve the record for the "furthest south" at 88° 23 ′ south. "A live donkey is better than a dead lion," said Shackleton to his wife Emily, in explanation of why he had decided to turn back.

Reinhold Messner, who has climbed all eight of the world's mountains over 8000 metres without oxygen, has said that when you know the mountain has won, it is time to turn back. Shackleton might equally have said that when you know the Barrier, the Beardmore, and the Polar Plateau have won, then one goes home; one returns to try again some other day.

To make a "brave retreat" demands a particular kind of courage – the ability to admit failure without suffering a loss of self-respect. It also requires a finely tuned consciousness – one employing the sharpest and most objective of sense perceptions to inform on the reality of the environmental situation, to reveal the full strength of the opposing forces. In addition, the protagonist's awareness must extend to a frank recognition of his or her own physical resources. Furthermore the imagination must come into play. In hazardous situations individuals must envisage – and mentally project themselves into – the challenges that lie ahead. These are the faculties that characterize a practical intelligence. And there is one more aspect of character – perhaps the most important – that plays a vital role in the "psychology of turning back": that of intuition – an immediate apprehension of the truth of a situation, mentally realized without conscious reasoning. Egotism cannot be a factor when the time comes to retreat. Men of Shackleton's ilk possess an inner strength and sense of self that does not have to be proved by *not* "giving in". To retreat when the odds are known is the mark of a spirit that transcends the needs of ego.

Now, in this soft, dreamy evening light, his hut has taken on a life of its own. Everything here – the pots, pans, tools . . . even the timbers – seems to have absorbed something of the intensity of daily life during the hut's occupation, the whole space seems to be a pressure cooker of signals and impressions from bygone days. I cannot satisfactorily describe the experience, except to say that on this particular evening Shackleton's hut is not simply an historic building – remote and generally inaccessible – but a real home charged with the spirit of the men who once lived in it. It feels as if things might still be going on there – as if Shackleton or Mawson might appear at any moment and start dusting off the snow.

Shackleton's hut – interior. "They are shadowy figures, quite silent, lumbering awkwardly from the inner porch to bend over sledges, make last-minute adjustments to each other's clothing, stamping their feet soundlessly in the last nervous moments before getting under way."
Photo: Colin Monteath

I never move from my corner, yet my mind is drifting – in among the group surrounding the four men of the polar team who are preparing to set out across the sea ice to reach the Barrier and commence their journey to the Pole.

They are shadowy figures, quite silent, lumbering awkwardly from the inner porch to bend over sledges, make last-minute adjustments to each other's clothing, stamping their feet soundlessly in the last nervous moments before getting under way. They start beneath a cloudless sky, the wind at their backs, coming from the north: good auguries at the beginning of the most testing journey in the world. Shackleton's presence is magnetic: he fairly crackles with energy and confidence as he moves over to talk to David, Mawson, and Mackay who are off to the unknown interior of Victoria Land. Inside the hut, peering into the cold space, I sense their hallucinatory presence as patches of darkness move back and forth across the threshold.

Raymond Priestley, Scott's geologist in 1910–13, had been with Shackleton on the 1908 expedition. He sledged over to Cape Royds one day to check up on the old hut. He and two others – one being Campbell, who was to lead Scott's Northern Party – stayed overnight. Here is a short extract from Priestley's account of the visit.

> On the shelves of my cubicle are still stacked the magazines and paper brought down by the relief ship. Nothing is changed at all except the company . . . I expect to see people come in through the door after a walk over the surrounding hills . . .
>
> The whole place is very eerie, there is such a feeling of life about it. Not only do I feel it, but the others do also. Last night after I turned in I could have sworn that I heard people shouting to each other.
>
> I thought that I had only got an attack of nerves, but Campbell asked me if I had heard any shouting, for he had certainly done so. It must have been the seals calling to each other, but it certainly did sound most human.

That so many decades later I should run into the same kind of strange phenomenon seems to suggest that whatever forces prevail in that place manage to be both dynamic and constant. The power of the imagination is strong – but I'm sure it can only work because the atmosphere of the hut is so vibrantly alive, still charged with the spirit of men who had carried out one of the most celebrated forays into the Antarctic wilderness.

OPPOSITE: *The Barne Glacier. "... here we are with this magnificent wall of ice stretching ahead for several miles beyond Cape Royds ..."* Photo: Neelon Crawford

5

SCOTT'S LAST EXPEDITION

A short run of eight miles down the Ross Island coast from Sir Ernest Shackleton's base at Cape Royds brings us to the Barne Glacier. For a moment I think we must somehow have reversed direction and are running alongside the Barrier again – which should now be some eighty miles behind us, just around the corner, so to speak, from Cape Bird. But here we are with this magnificent wall of ice stretching ahead for several miles beyond Cape Royds to Cape Evans – the site of Captain Robert Falcon Scott's base camp.

The hut at Cape Evans was erected in 1911 to house the men of Scott's *Terra Nova* expedition – *Terra Nova* being the name of the old Scottish whaler of some 700 tons which transported them to McMurdo Sound.

Cape Evans – at the tip of one of the spurs of Mount Erebus – was named after Lieutenant Teddy Evans, second-in-command of the expedition and master of the *Terra Nova*.

Cape Evans lies about twenty-five miles north of the Barrier's edge, where New Zealand and the United States now maintain their bases. Travel overland between the two places is extremely difficult as glacial tongues and craggy terrain make it hazardous and slow going. Nowadays helicopters make light of the distance, but in Scott's day the journey to the Barrier was made either by sled over stable winter sea ice, or by taking the ship south through open-water leads when they existed. Cape Evans – for obvious reasons – had been known as "The Skuary" by the members of Scott's earlier 1902 expedition which had been based further south at Hut Point, close to the Barrier. But when *Terra Nova* arrived off Ross Island in 1911, sea ice blocked the way south to Hut Point; consequently, "The Skuary" was chosen as the site for the later expedition and renamed Cape Evans.

The new hut – built to house the party of thirty-one men through two Antarctic winters – was much grander than Shackleton's hut at Cape Royds: much larger, more solidly constructed, and more thoroughly insulated. The New Zealand Antarctic people who now maintain the site obviously do their best to keep the interior of the building looking as it did in Scott's day. Every bunk still has its reindeer skin sleeping bag, shelves are littered with apparatus and personal effects, scientific work in progress (penguin dissection, for example) remains in place – while pots and pans and tins of food litter stove and table tops. In this respect, the hut is as effective a record of Antarctic exploration a hundred years ago as was Shackleton's. Yet, it seems to carry nothing of the spirit of the past, despite the fact that it was home to the men of the expedition for almost three years – a lengthy sojourn which came to an end with the discovery of the bodies of Scott, Wilson, and Bowers on the Barrier. It is as if the place has been crushed beneath the burden of the tragedy it has come to represent.

A glaciologist from Switzerland, on leaving the hut, expressed it concisely. "It's not a memorial," he said, "it's a tomb."

It is a sad and well-known story – and one which makes the hut at Cape Evans the most famous of all bases in the history of Antarctic exploration. Scott and four companions had successfully reached the South Pole on 17 January 1912 after a journey which had severely taxed them physically

Scott's Hut. "It is as if the place has been crushed beneath the burden of the tragedy it has come to represent." Photo: Colin Monteath

before they even reached the heights of the Antarctic Plateau, via the Beardmore Glacier, to proceed the remaining 400-odd miles to the Pole. When they finally attained their goal, it was to discover that Roald Amundsen had beaten them to it by a few short weeks.

Weather conditions on the return were terrible – blizzards kept them in their tent for days at a time. Petty Officer Evans died, and was buried at the foot of the Beardmore Glacier. On 16 March, when they were in the middle of the Barrier, and on the day before his thirty-second birthday, Captain Lawrence Oates walked out of the tent to his death in a raging blizzard, knowing that gangrene had finally overcome his frostbitten feet. This act of Oates to go out from the tent in order not to further slow the party's progress, is surely one of the most famous events in Antarctic history. Yet nobody who knew "Soldier" – as he was affectionately called –

would be surprised by his decision to walk willingly to his death in order to give his comrades a greater chance of survival. For at this point, not only his feet, but his hands also, were terribly frostbitten. It was taking him almost two hours to put his footgear on. The pain must have been intolerable. In fact, his feet had been giving him trouble for over two months, yet he had concealed the problem; kept on the skis, kept pulling his load. On his last morning, the weather still blizzarding, he simply said, "I am just going outside and I may be some time." He was not seen again. The story of Oates's life is that of a brave man, a man of sardonic outlook balanced by a strong sense of humour. He was his "own man" in every sense of the term.

Scott, Wilson, and Bowers made their last camp on the Barrier approximately 125 miles from Hut Point, and only eleven miles from a food depot which they were unable to reach. They had been away from base, on the ice, for five months. It was not until eight months later that their bodies, together with diaries and letters, were found by a search team of their colleagues from Cape Evans. The tent was collapsed over them and a cairn of snow blocks piled upon their frail and fallen shelter.

I stand around for a while on the black sand after leaving Scott's hut, my spirits momentarily low, trying to decide in which direction to set off alone for a recuperative walk. Life in the Antarctic is both cruel and vicious, yet perhaps no more so than anywhere else in the world. The game of life and death is going on everywhere, all the time in nature. But in the Antarctic summer it is starkly out in the open: there is no vegetation, no dark night or dim and shady place to hide it from view. It is a white world where the clarity of the air allows the eye to pick up the slightest movement, the slightest hint of a darker tone, even at great distances. There is no disguising the harsh reality; nowhere to go to escape it.

I decide to walk south along the snowbound ledges and scree in the general direction of the Erebus Ice Tongue, keeping the partially frozen coastal stretches of the Sound on my right. It is easy going if one avoids the larger tracts of snow which could conceal the deeper gullies and irregularities of the terrain. After the Cape Royds experience I give the colonies of skuas along the way a wide berth: they are easily picked out for they choose clusters of the largest boulders on which to breed, and they always seem to have one or two guards posted on the higher and most visible positions. I am about half a mile along before I clear their outposts.

The overall silence is numbing – blunting all the senses: an object lesson on how difficult it must be to adjust to a totally silent world. I jump, startled out of my wits, when the stillness is broken by the late-summer crackings of sea ice still struggling to break loose, and sounding like pistol shots tearing into the brittle Antarctic air.

The rock is hard on the feet. Turning to regard the sprawling bulk of the volcano smoking behind me I can't believe it is almost 13,000 feet high. From this vantage point it looks almost squat, truncated. Not only is it difficult to judge the size of things, but also to estimate the lapse of time since starting out. Despite the need to stay alert, such concerns don't seem to register fully in this thousands-of-miles-from-anywhere white wilderness where day does not really become night. Across the water a large chunk of tabular iceberg is jammed fast against the cliff of a hump-backed island of rock, completely dwarfing its captor. The parent berg must have broken free and drifted off on its northern journey some time ago. It must have been enormous. You could still level a runway and land a medium-sized jet on what remains of it.

I am acutely aware of this place as the only virginal continent left – except, of course, for the scientists who too often think of it as their own. I try to imagine what will happen if oil and mineral exploration ever become a reality, what would happen to the whales, seals, penguins, birds, and, more than likely, the world's climate. Already, human beings have begun to alter the fragile ecology of the continent, at least along the vital coastline. Even the scientists, those who should be most concerned with preserving this wondrous natural laboratory, disrupt and contaminate their surroundings, often, it seems, with little concern for the consequences. For a time at their McMurdo Station the Americans created a garbage dump on the ice nearly a mile long, expecting that it would just float away and disintegrate with its junk in the Ross Sea. Happily, now, like the New Zealanders, they are despatching their waste to New Zealand. Even so, in the summer McMurdo becomes a "frontier town" supporting perhaps 1200 personnel: too many people in one place in this fragile environment.

Now the Japanese are harvesting krill in very substantial quantities as quality protein for the dog-and-cat-food industry. What will happen, one wonders, to the Antarctic fauna – the penguins, seals and whales, whose existence depends on this fundamental food source. The Japanese, too, are still whaling, taking several hundred whales each year – all, they say, in the interest of science.

Like the environment of the desert, that of the Antarctic is remarkably fragile. The number of species, the biodiversity, is small, the food chain very short. Serious wounding cannot be easily healed – the conditions are simply too harsh to permit rapid or substantial recovery.

In front of me a projecting shelf of black rock, much higher on the slope, but seemingly only a few hundred yards ahead, catches my eye. It would provide an ideal vantage point for overlooking both the Sound and the volcano. After fifteen minutes of cautious progress I look up and see that nothing has changed. The ledge ahead does not appear to be any closer.

It's the air, I say to myself, remembering how easily the eyes can be deceived by this incredibly pure and brittle-clear atmosphere. I remind myself, too, of how quickly and unexpectedly the weather can change, recalling accounts in the journals of Antarctic explorers of blizzards descending in minutes, zero visibility, and dangerous drops in temperature, even in summer. Yet I keep walking, telling myself I will turn back at the ledge. Why I should persist in such a reckless fashion is difficult to defend. Although I am mentally registering landmarks, and noting the angle of my climb away from the corner of the large stranded iceberg, I have no sense of the distance I have travelled. Perhaps I am being driven by a need to experience something of the kind of solitude Antarctic explorers wrote about; to take on – in my own small way – the challenge of this starkly beautiful, but treacherous place. Even so, I go cautiously, picking a way carefully to avoid large areas of snow, keeping on bare rock or scree where there are no hidden pitfalls. I have no idea of the time: stopped wearing a watch weeks ago.

Things below me are now hidden by the slope of the terrain; but finally real progress is being made toward the ledge which looms ever closer until, suddenly, it jumps stereoscopically forward to present itself not as a ledge, but a small black basalt cliff about seven feet high, capped with a mush-rooming overhang of ice. The summit of Erebus is just visible, partially screened by the now steeply rising ground – seemingly a short afternoon stroll away carrying a bag of watercress sandwiches. Only now do I realize I have ventured on to the side of the volcano – for the slope above my mini-cliff is composed of a wide swath of high rock-and-ice cones, the bases of which connect with each other to form deep basins which have the appearance of shell holes created by a heavy artillery barrage. Higher still the rising ground gives way to the glistening overhangs and semi-caves of icefalls. Time to stop.

Sitting on a flat stone, back and shoulders wedged comfortably against the cliff wall, I let my eyes wander slowly over the desolate but striking panorama spread before me. Far below, strips of coastal ice spear the black water, while to the south Glacier Tongue appears from behind a headland, seeming to extend for two or three miles into McMurdo Sound. Its walls sparkle in the sun like a giant reflecting mirror, spilling blue and green lights into the atmosphere and over the sea like a firework display. Off to the north the roof of Scott's hut is just visible, lost in the immensity of the space. Seen from this height, the shape of Erebus's moraine-like spur which forms Cape Evans is well-defined. And I realize that to describe Antarctica simply as a *white* wilderness is inaccurate. At least near the coast, there is much exposed rock which acts as a dark foil to the white ground; while the snow itself, as well as the ice, becomes iridescent, gleaming with pockets of soft blue and subtle blushes of rose which blend into the transparent air of summer.

The fact that weather conditions are ideal for my solitary trek – I can see seventy or so miles across the Sound to the dry valleys of the 10,000-foot-high mountains of the Royal Society Range – no doubt contributes to this new chromatic sensitivity on my part: the subtle play of light, the refraction of colour, is quite extraordinary.

I spot a skua flying leisurely up from the sea, heading in my direction. After flying in wide circles above my head – with no hint of menace – the bird touches down on a jumble of volcanic rock no further than twelve feet away; then turning to face me, it pulls itself up as high as possible without actually having to take off, craning its head upward to stretch the muscles of its broad and powerful breast – proceeding to extend one wing then the other toward the sky at an angle of 45°, before settling comfortably into the rock, wings furled and feet tucked away. The skua seems quite content in my company, and I must admit to feeling privileged at being so accepted.

There was an entry in Edward Wilson's journal which described a skua flying overhead when he, together with the rest of Scott's party, were at latitude 87° 20´ south on the high Antarctic Plateau only some 150 miles from the Pole. He wrote that it was ". . . evidently hungry but not weak. Its droppings were clear mucus, nothing in them at all. It appeared in the afternoon and disappeared again about half-an-hour later."

What on earth could the bird have been up to – flying at such an altitude above the Polar Plateau, at least 600 miles from its prime feeding ground, the sea; with no penguin rookery nearer than the southernmost Adélie colony at Cape Royds to provide chicks or eggs for sustenance? Was it lost? Blown across from East Antarctica by a south-moving blizzard? Whatever the reasons, the Ancient Greeks would surely have seen its presence as a sign – and especially when its droppings were found to contain no nutrients.

They would have been right, of course, as things turned out. Look what happened on Scott's return journey.

I push hard against the ledge wall, staring at my skua. Even sitting with wings furled, the long, curved beak singles him out for attention. A true bird of omen. If only Scott could have divined the significance of theirs.

Scott and Wilson wrote letters home before they died – moving last thoughts which were recovered by the search party some eight months later when the Antarctic spring came round again. They were missives displaying the great courage with which they accepted the end – serene, almost, in the Christian sentiments which were expressed: duty had been performed and now, in faith, it was a matter of waiting for God's Will to be done. Scott asked that the country should look well after their next-of-kin.

I sit wondering at the strength of faith, the dignity and quiet manner which attended the deaths of these men – for although I gather they possessed opium pills as a means to take their own lives, they preferred to die naturally. It is surely impressive that the values and virtues of middle-class Edwardian England carried them through what might well be considered the most hazardous journey in the world. Yet that ingrained British respect for the amateur – for understatement, and for participating in the game of life as a "gentleman player" rather than training to become a "real pro" – might well have cost Scott and his party their lives. Such a philosophy was nourished by the idea that strength of will and spirit – moral fibre, so called – was only developed by putting oneself to the severest of tasks, pushing body and mind to extreme limits and trusting in God to see one through: and that this is how the Almighty would have it. Take this principle to its logical conclusion and it can be seen how it could promote, perhaps subliminally, a certain cavalier enthusiasm in tackling dangerous and difficult missions – an attitude which tends to both distrust and eschew the application of specialized knowledge and the honing of necessary skills because, if one removes some degree of danger and hardship from the task, by so doing, the challenge to moral and physical strength is diminished, rendering success less worthy.

Nowadays, I think – watching the skua preen himself – it is unlikely that any vestige of such metaphysical amateurism would pervade the minds of Antarctic scientists (the contemporary explorers), even were modern technological aids not so supreme. Reliance on a thorough professionalism and specialization is the order of the day. A sense of the sublime no doubt has its place – but after the fact, after the accomplishment of the mission: such as being moved by seeing the beauty of planet earth from the moon, for example.

As I sit up on my vantage point, identifying with this historic site and all that went on here almost 100 years ago, it seems incongruous that one would import God into such an elemental place – a God, that is, which is so anthropomorphized through centuries of involvement in human affairs as to have questionable significance in a land which has known no human history, which has bred not one indigenous man or woman. Consequently, the myth you bring with you – shaped by custom and convention – is not elemental enough to work in this timeless land. For it is the promise of this place that one might find the old imperishable and antediluvian spirit deep within the self. Oates went out into the blizzard knowing that the time had come to face it. "That's the challenge and the appeal, isn't it?" I say aloud to the skua who turns away to look out to sea. He is obviously not impressed. Why should he be? He's a professional in matters of life down here.

Now Roald Amundsen the Norwegian was a professional – an expert on snow and ice who had wintered over eleven times in polar regions, and who gathered together a team of similarly experienced men: he chose men who were expert in using skis for long distance cross-country travel, and could handle Greenland dogs used to sledge hauling. (Nansen, the Norwegian pioneer explorer, advised Scott against using ponies in such a fierce climate, over such terrible terrain; Scott's decision to do so ensured that it would finally be the men themselves who hauled supplies for most of the journey.) Amundsen's team trained, practised, and planned for every contingency; yet were still prepared to take two vital chances – establishing a base camp on the moving Ross Ice Shelf, and pioneering a new and hitherto unknown route to the Pole over the Axel-Heiberg Glacier. I would guess, too, that he left the God back home out of it. And he succeeded.

Sitting high and isolated beneath the ledge, looking down on the coastal sea ice over which Scott and his ten-man, ten-pony team headed south for the Barrier on 1 November 1911, I am able more completely to comprehend the full reality of Shackleton's, Scott's, and Amundsen's achievements of almost a century ago. This detached perch on Erebus accomplishes what Scott's hut could not do – that is, engage the mind and nerve of a novice to understand something of what Scott and his companions endured on their dreadful journey. It forces one to feel for them as they heaved heavy sledges over broken and unstable ice where treacherous snow-bridges could collapse and drop them hundreds of feet into the abyss; or as they scaled the steep and treacherous icefalls of the glacier. At the same time, they had to deal with the terrible summer weather that year, erecting tents in gale force winds, marching during the long days of blizzards dragging loaded sledges, and suffering sub-zero temperatures at night; all the while living with an ever-increasing hunger, the food available proving inadequate for the time they were out; finally being faced with a shortage of fuel for heating and cooking . . . leading to starvation and a freezing death.

Up to and until the return there had been hope. When the last support group left them at the top of the Beardmore to return to Cape Evans, the remaining five – it should have been four, but Scott added Bowers at the last minute – faced the final slog to the Pole over the high plateau knowing it was finally within reach. They arrived on 17 January 1912 – two and a half months after leaving Cape Evans – only to find Amundsen's tent and a message for the Norwegian king. The effect of this discovery on morale must have been profound. Now they had to get back – psychological resources considerably dented, physical ones already stretched to the limit.

A gust of wind from high on the volcano swoops over the ledge at my back, whining like a warning siren activated by a sudden surge of power. Erebus can make its own weather. It would be wise to start back down.

I can't drag my thoughts away from Scott's men. Grim pictures keep coming to mind: the struggle up the Beardmore; reaching the Pole only to catch sight of the fluttering black marker flag which Amundsen had tied to a sledge bearer: huddling together in the tent, trapped by the long blizzard which ended their lives. I feel a terrible aching sorrow, despite the years that have passed since their tragic journey.

Inevitably I ponder the differences between Shackleton and Scott. It is not possible to fault either in terms of bravery and courage. (Scott, on one occasion – and against all advice – had himself lowered some sixty feet into a crevasse to rescue one of the dogs that had fallen on to a narrow ledge.) No: it becomes a matter of background and temperament.

Shackleton – who came to a life at sea by way of the Merchant Marine and had seen much of the world before turning to Antarctic exploration possessed a genuine affinity for the Antarctic wilderness and the dangerous challenges it offered. He followed his own highly personal way of seeing things – was very much his own man – depending neither on institutions or traditions to help form his opinions or influence his actions. Given to both reading and quoting poetry during his bridge watches at sea – Robert Browning being his favourite poet – Ernest Shackleton was a man capable of quick and ready insight. There was something of the Celtic dreamer about him that suggests an undercover awareness at work, an absorbed contact with a deep inner intelligence. He knew when to wait patiently, and when to grasp the nettle and act. And when he did act it was with resolution, fortitude, and faith in his own powers. His men were prepared to trust him, both when it was a matter of waiting and when it was time for action. He was not the best of planners, and at times none too realistic as to what an expedition could achieve. But when things went wrong and the going got rough, there was surely no more inspired a leader.

Scott, well-meaning and liked by most of his company, was a Royal Naval captain inured to the rigidity of that service's way of thinking and copybook way of doing things. Motivated by a strong sense of patriotism – Britain first to the South Pole – and not unmindful of the career prospects offered by Antarctic exploration, he obviously considered the British way of tackling difficult and unfamiliar problems (sometimes called "muddling through") to be the best. The sort of natural, intuitive intelligence which allows a leader to "sniff out" the steps to follow and foresee the consequences down the line, does not seem to have been one of Scott's gifts. There are many unanswered questions about Scott's last expedition, not the least being that if Scott had not given Wilson permission in 1911 to undertake the gruelling trek to study the emperors, prior to the Polar trek proper, might it have made a difference to the outcome of the Polar journey?

I find myself thinking about Wilson, Bowers, and Cherry-Garrard. I wonder how they lived through that horrendous *winter* journey from Cape Evans to Cape Crozier: rounding Ross Island by means of the sea ice and

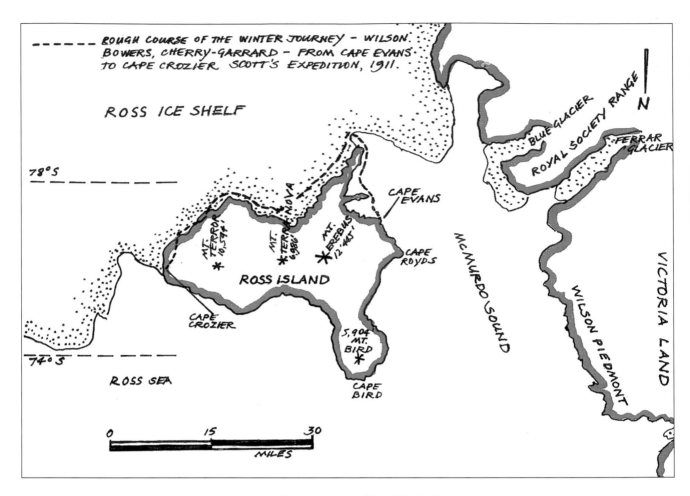

Ross Island and McMurdo Sound

then up and over the Barrier – pressure ridges with their deep runnels on the frozen sea, crevasses on the ice shelf – all in twenty-four-hour darkness. And the constant blizzarding, day and night, temperatures dropping to –60°C and moving but little higher during the day. Yet, after it all, they were the first to see an emperor penguin colony in mid-winter, the breeding season for these birds, and to bring back three eggs for scientific research. It was a seventy-mile journey each way – the outward leg alone taking three weeks – and in conditions previously thought endurable for only a few days at a time. In his classic book *The Worst Journey in the World*, Cherry-Garrard described how their clothes froze, encasing them in a suit of armour made of ice. At the outset his sleeping bag weighed 8 kilograms (18 lbs), yet on returning to Cape Evans its weight was 20 kilograms (45 lb) – the difference due to accumulated ice.

None of them was specially trained for these conditions. Dr Edward Wilson – physician, scientist, ornithologist, and skilled artist who would

Head of an emperor. "... they were the first to see an emperor penguin colony in mid-winter ..."

draw and record things even in the grimmest of conditions and who was Scott's right-hand man, and also a close friend of Shackleton – was always out in front on the Cape Crozier expedition, testing the ground for the others. "Birdie" Bowers, the Scot, with his great beak of a nose, short and barrel-chested, was as strong as a horse. He was resourceful under pressure – no task being too difficult – never seemed to tire, was always optimistic, and proved himself an indispensable organizer of equipment and jack-of-all trades. Apsley George Benet Cherry-Garrard himself came from a wealthy background; he studied History and Classics at Oxford, donated £1000 to Scott's expedition and was taken on as assistant geologist. He was probably the least prepared of the three for the winter journey and suffered excruciating hardship. Yet he showed not a scrap of self-pity, simply an extraordinary capacity to grin and bear it. He remained deeply affected by the tragedy of Scott for the rest of his life, and years later reflected on how he regretted that "the values of gentlemanly altruism were becoming increasingly lost in the modern world."

Wilson and Bowers had barely three months to recover from that trek before embarking on the long slog to the Pole and back. If they had been

Mt Erebus by moonlight. "... given the phenomenal variations of atmospheric density and light around Erebus one can never be certain about what such a local system might do – engulf the mountainside or disappear altogether ..."

Photo: Colin Monteath

in tip-top physical condition – particularly so in the case of Bowers – the eleven miles to One Ton Depot with its food and fuel might have been covered, and might they not then have had the strength to carry on?

The skua alongside my perch is on its feet. The wave of cold air descending from Erebus has subsided, leaving a deep chill in its wake. From the look of the sky it could be quite late in the day: pale blue has given way to a dull chrome-green that takes on the lustre of pewter where it falls behind the mountains of the Royal Society Range across the water. Now there is no illusion as to distance: the range and its dry valleys seem a long way off – the full seventy miles. With the sun's light dimming behind these western mountains the upper slopes of Erebus are lost in a pale white haze which spreads over the summit, a delicately formed, semitransparent cloud of indeterminate outline which bleeds away into the surrounding sky. Is it stationary? I can't be sure: given the phenomenal variations of atmospheric density and light around Erebus one can never be certain about what such a local system might do – engulf the mountain-side or disappear altogether, and all in the space of a few minutes.

The skua is flexing first one wing then the other before finally taking to the air. It is obviously time to go. I watch him disappear beneath the slope of the mountainside.

I start down myself, retracing my footprints in the snow until confronted by a wide expanse of steeply inclined ledge-outcrop and scree. Here the ground is swept clear of snow, and with no tracks to follow I abruptly find myself strangely disoriented: without warning I am completely overcome by the enormity of the surrounding space; normal perceptions of the lie of the land are lost. For a few moments I can't even determine from which direction I've come, never mind in which direction I should proceed to reach Scott's hut – what is the correct angle of descent to follow. And then, far below, I see the skuas fluttering over their rocks.

6

THE HOME OF THE
BLIZZARD

WITH CAMPBELL AND MAWSON SOUTH AND
WEST OF CAPE ADARE

On a Sunday morning we are in McMurdo Sound, off Cape Evans, and the killer whales are with us.

I must admit to a dislike of the killer whale (*Orcinus orca*), not because I have strong feelings against predators but because this one, which is among the most successful of all, is too often marketed to us as being harmless and even benign. A number of people even oppose using the term "killer whale", their argument being that they have never attacked a human being. They cannot have read the diaries and accounts of Antarctic explorers.

Scott's second expedition had an extraordinary encounter with them, related by Cherry-Garrard in *The Worst Journey in the World*. Quoting from Scott's own diaries, he described it as "the adventure of Ponting and the Killer Whales".

I was a little late on the scene this morning, and thereby witnessed a most extraordinary scene. Some six or seven killer whales, old and young, were skirting the fast floe edge ahead of the ship; they seemed excited and dived rapidly, almost touching the floe. As we watched, they suddenly appeared astern, raising their snouts out of water. I had heard weird stories of these beasts, but had never associated real danger with them. Close to the water's edge lay the wire stern rope of the ship, and our two Esquimaux dogs were tethered to this. I did not think of connecting the movement of the whales with this fact, and seeing them so close I shouted to Ponting, who was standing abreast of the ship. He seized his camera and ran towards the floe edge to get a close picture of the beasts, which had momentarily disappeared. The next moment the whole floe under him and the dogs heaved up and split into fragments. One could hear the booming noise as the whales rose under the ice and struck it with their backs. Whale after whale rose under the ice, setting it rocking fiercely; luckily Ponting kept his feet and was able to fly to security. By an extraordinary chance also, the splits had been made around and between the dogs, so that neither of them fell into the water. Then it was clear that the whales shared our astonishment, for one after another their huge hideous heads shot vertically into the air through the cracks which they had made. As they reared them to a height of six or eight feet it was possible to see their tawny head markings, their small glistening eyes, and their terrible array of teeth – by far the largest and most terrifying in the world. There cannot be a doubt that they looked up to see what had happened to Ponting and the dogs.

Nor can the opponents of the title "killer" have seen the frightful film of an army of killer whales, perhaps twenty or so, slashing and tearing at a great blue whale, the largest creature on earth. I say "army" because the attack was carried out with military precision with each individual seemingly assigned a specific area of attack – flukes, flanks, fins, etc. Those near the head would dive beneath it to prevent it from escaping. As the orcas are unable to dive as deeply as the blue it was necessary for them to keep it on or near the surface.

The attack continued for what seemed an eternity – fifteen, twenty minutes, perhaps even half-an-hour. Then, suddenly, it was over and, as quickly as they had come, they vanished. The explanation given by the observing scientists was that this had been probably a "training exercise" for the younger orcas: that the intention, on this occasion was not to kill, but to practise killing. In all probability, however, the blue whale would eventually die. It seemed almost impossible that this huge creature left floating alone on the surface of the Pacific could survive the terrible wounds which had been inflicted upon it.

Orcas were certainly as much feared by the Indians of the Pacific Northwest, an area well-known for large concentrations of orcas, as they were by Antarctic explorers. Even today at the American bases instructions are given to personnel going out in Zodiacs to seek land immediately upon sighting orcas in the vicinity. They will, as so succinctly stated in one book, "kill everything in the ocean larger than a shrimp."*

A pod of fifty or more orcas are racing across the mirror-like surface of the Sound. Caught in the still reflection of Mount Erebus, their high, vertical dorsal fins – identifying them as males – look like the periscopes of fast moving submarines. They never for a moment are deflected from their course – straight and fast like torpedoes they come until, reaching the starboard side of the ship, they slip one by one beneath it to emerge on the other side, close to the edge of the ice.

The specific name orca may be derived from *Orcus*, an ancient god of the Roman underworld so old that the Romans probably shared him with the Etruscans. Erebus is from the Greek *Erebos*, the personification of darkness or a place of darkness in the underworld. On this brilliant sunlit morning the gods of death are at play on a wide and frozen sea.

The gods of the weather also appear to be in a benign mood. Yet I am not too sanguine when it comes to thinking how we might fare in the next two days. A freshening wind is coming off the slopes of Erebus, and I remember the comment of one Antarctic scientist at the Scott Polar Institute in Cambridge always to be concerned about any weather coming from the south. "If you're lucky enough to have reasonable seas and weather all the way through to McMurdo, you'll not get away with it on the way out. Never seen the glass fall as quickly as it does in that part of the world. You can have a force 10 at your back in no time at all."

In thirty-six hours or less, heading north from Cape Evans for New Zealand, we will be in the notorious seas which make the approaches to Cape Adare so hazardous. And I don't fancy the possibility of a Polar gale coming at us from behind.

It is along this glaciated coastline where we are to sail – the coast between McMurdo Sound and Cape Adare – that Scott's Northern Party under Commander Victor Campbell took to the sea ice in the hope of returning to Cape Evans.

It had all begun on 26 January 1911, when the six men of the Northern Party made their farewells to Scott and the others. Circumstances ultimately dictated that changes be made in their original plan – that of exploring King Edward VII Land which lay beyond the eastern flank of

---

* Balcomb, Kenneth C. III, *The Whales of Hawaii*, a publication of the Marine Mammal Fund 1987.

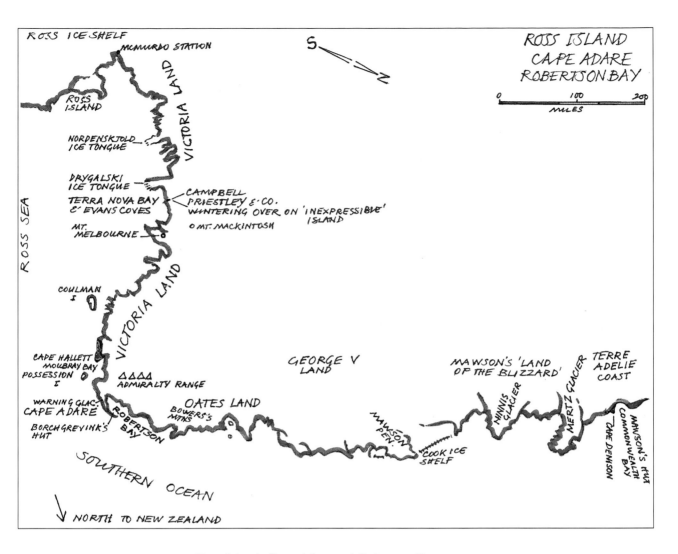

Ross Island, Cape Adare and Robertson Bay

the Ross Ice Shelf – for on *Terra Nova*'s arrival in the area Campbell discovered that Amundsen was already there: his ship *Fram*, was occupying the only safe anchorage in the region. Returning to Cape Evans with the news about Amundsen, Campbell turned his attention to northern Victoria Land and Cape Adare, and *Terra Nova* finally landed the party at Robertson Bay on the west side of the Cape, together with hut and supplies.

From there the Northern Party carried out a normal winter programme, even getting out in very early spring to attempt exploratory surveys of the Victoria Land coastline. *Terra Nova* returned from New Zealand to pick them up on 3 January 1912, but instead of sailing directly back to Cape Evans, Campbell – who had been somewhat frustrated by the limitations of sledge travel away from base imposed by the geography of the Cape

Adare region – decided to leave the ship and establish a depot at Evans Coves in Terra Nova Bay. From there they would spend six weeks exploring the glaciers of the region and the surrounds of Mount Melbourne to the north, returning to the depot in time to meet the ship and be taken out around 18 February.

So the stage was set for the adventure that was to follow – the adventure described so graphically by Raymond Priestley (later to become Sir Raymond Priestley) in his *Antarctic Adventure: Scott's Northern Party:* "Marooned at the stormiest place in Victoria Land in this the stormiest recorded year in Antarctic history, we spent eight months living in a hole in the snow on one month's sledging provisions and what we could pick up locally, and in summer clothes. It was an experience that might have broken the strongest team. That we survived, most of us in good fettle, was largely due to our leader's quality."

The group had waited vainly for the ship on the ice and moraine of Evans Coves, and did so in terrible early autumn weather: high winds, thick with snow, were the order of the day for much of the time. They were not to know that *Terra Nova* had made three attempts to reach them, but had encountered impenetrable pack ice twenty-seven miles out – and finally had to sail away – because from their vantage point the bay itself was clear of ice and, in Priestley's words, "lashed to fury by the wind".

Raymond Priestley was the only civilian among the explorers, the others being Royal Navy men: Victor Campbell and Murray Levick (Naval Surgeon) – both officers – together with Petty Officers George Abbott and Frank Browning, and Able Seaman Harry Dickason.

Gales continued into early March, and before the first week of the month was out they knew they must plan to hole up for the coming winter, in the hope of then sledging south to Cape Evans in the spring. Their summer tents were already holed and provided little protection against the wind under present conditions, never mind those that could be expected in the coming winter. An ice cave was the only answer. And a hunting party must be out constantly looking for seals and penguins in order to build up a winter larder.

The spot chosen in which to dig the cave was a large snowdrift which had built-up alongside a granite outcrop running into the boulder-strewn shore. They called it Inexpressible Island. Priestley wrote: "On the 5th [of March] although the gale continued, it was free from snow, and we were just able to make our way over the ridge at the back of our camp and into the next valley where the bigger of the two snowdrifts was situated, and three of us commenced to dig into this drift. This work was continued during most of the days which followed, and as we made the cave larger and larger the wind worried us less and less except on our journeys to and from the drift. We first sank a trench 3 feet by 4 feet to a depth of 6 feet, and then from the side of this we picked out a large cave towards the thickest part of the drift."

When finished, the floor was covered with pebbles, insulation against the frozen ground being provided by dried seaweed. In area the cave was 12′ by 9′ having a height of 5′ 6″. The entrance way was so low that it required crawling in and out on hands and knees. They spent much of the winter lying in their sleeping bags, as their blubber-grimed rags of clothing permitted but brief forays to look for seals or penguins and obey the calls of nature. Their diet was basically seal and penguin and thick strips of raw blubber. Cooking on the primus in such a confined space imparted a dark oily coating to every surface – "smitch" as they called it (a more expressive term than smoke), which irritated and reddened the eyes acutely, even resulting in "smitch-blindness". To relieve the darkness and conserve fuel they fabricated a blubber-burning light using frayed string and rope as a wick: four of these were in constant use throughout the twenty-four hours of winter darkness. One can fully appreciate Priestley's claim that they made all the difference between surviving or going under.

Levick, the surgeon, instituted a regimen of "Swedish" exercises – a pulling and stretching of arms, trunk, and abdomen to prevent wastage of muscle and sinew for when it came time to undertake the march to Cape Evans. As they were not able to stand upright in their "igloo" an observer would likely have found it a droll sight. Also, every night, Levick would read one chapter from one of the three books they had with them: Dickens's *David Copperfield*, for example, lasted them for some sixty nights. They devised endless ways and rituals to "make a life" under such conditions: celebrating birthdays and other notable calendar dates with the distribution of a few raisins, an extra sugar lump, or a piece of chocolate from the depot of carefully hoarded sledging rations, together with singsongs and the practice of maintaining regular and normal conversations.

For seven months they lived in this way, leaving the cave as infrequently as possible. The contemporary reader of Priestley's chronicle cannot but be amazed – if not awed – how, despite the bouts of depression and the dysenteric illnesses from which they suffered, and which almost killed Browning and Dickason, these six men developed such a serenity and equanimity as a true and caring community. The expression, "One for all and all for one", takes on new meaning through the pages of Priestley's book.

On 30 September the men left their ice-cave winter quarters for the 200-mile trek to Cape Evans, much of it over a totally unknown terrain of coastal mountain range and fractured sea ice – the very coast, in fact, alongside which we are about to sail heading for Cape Adare. The tents and sleeping bags had been patched and all depot supplies loaded on two sledges. Browning was completely incapacitated with enteritis and Dickason fifty percent so. Priestley commented: "We have been reduced to 4½ pulling units . . ." They were forty days on the march, and without Levick's care Browning would not have survived. There were days when the high ridges and deep valleys of the glaciers reduced the distance they travelled to but two or three miles; days when the coastal ice was pressured into wavelike crests and troughs six feet high over which the loaded sledges must be hauled and then let down, time and time again – hard pulling for weakened stomachs.

Here's Priestley on the crossing of the Drygalski Ice Tongue, after the whole party, sledges and all, had almost fallen into a deep chasm the night before:

> We have had another gruelling day over a succession of ice-waves from 40 to 50 feet high, with their broken crests facing the south. Every now and then one of these ends in a sheer cliff-face, and the valley becomes almost a gorge with one or two, usually one, steep faces. We have only had to relay once during the day, but after our experience of last night we prospected the descent into the troughs of the waves with Alpine rope before we ventured into them with the sledges, and this has taken up a good deal of time.

Mirages, especially approaching the Nordenskjold Ice Tongue – one more seaward extending barrier – were particularly stressful. The fifty-foot-high walls of ice would continually change shape ". . . sometimes appearing as jagged cliffs several hundred feet high, sometimes as cliff on cliff piled in the sky", while the intervening distance could never be accurately perceived. ". . . Hour after hour we toiled towards the wall, sometimes bringing it nearer apparently, and sometimes seeing it visibly receded into the distance."*

Once over the Drygalski, however, the men were travelling over sea ice that had been traversed by David and Mawson and members of Shackleton's Western Party on their way to locate the south magnetic pole in 1908. It was territory where the odd food depot had been laid – food which most likely saved Browning's life when Campbell, Priestley and companions were still some days out from Cape Evans. The story of these men's winter survival is remarkable enough in itself, yet it should also be remembered that before being marooned at Terra Nova Bay they had already spent one Antarctic winter in the land of wind and blizzard at Cape Adare.

At the moment, close to the coast along which Campbell and the Northern Party struggled to reach Cape Evans, the sea is clear of ice, yet the weather has changed dramatically. The breeze that was behind our backs at Cape Evans – coming off Erebus – has dropped. All is grey, airless and without that wonderful Antarctic light, as extracts from my log describe – some thirty hours out from Cape Evans.

3 pm. A grey pall of moisture-laden air hangs low over the sea. The cloud ceiling is barely a thousand feet, visibility a mile at most. Apart from the movement of air which we ourselves create, the entire world seems waxen and absolutely still. But now no open water is visible; yet the ice is young, no more than two to three inch pack, and we slide easily through it – a ghostlike ship on a ghostlike sea.

10 pm. Passing between Coulman Island and the mainland. Already there are murmurings of wind behind us coming from the south, the home of summer gales. Ice breaking up and water beginning to show signs of restlessness – some patchy local eddies and troughs are giving way to longer running swells.

---

* The mirage phenomena in the Antarctic are extraordinarily convincing. Commander Campbell once called for the binoculars to identify figures approaching, convinced they were men heliographing his party; a few minutes later the distant figures turned out to be a group of emperor penguins.

Coastline traversed by Scott's northern party. "… the entire world seems waxen and absolutely still." Photo: Colin Monteath

5.30 am. Rudely awakened by a vicious roll to port followed by a jarring lurch to starboard, The whine of the wind is audible in the cabin – while through the porthole the sea is streaked with spindrift, and waves about six feet high roll past the ship, heading north. Brief snow-flurries sweep by – visibility is no greater than half a mile. The barometer reads 994 millibars and the news from the bridge is that following winds from the South Pole are expected to reach force 7 (moderate to near gale) during the course of the morning.

8 am. The barometer has fallen a few more millibars, the wind increased to force 8 to 9, fresh to strong gale winds between forty-five and fifty-five miles per hour. The wind keeps veering to starboard, causing the vessel to trend toward Cape Hallett off the port bow. Strong right rudder is required to maintain our course and keep our distance from land.

11 am. We are in Mowbray Bay, and Possession Island lies somewhere ahead. It is snowing heavily with our limited visibility reduced even further. There are icebergs nearby, but they are becoming increasingly hard to see. We will pass well to the east of Possession Island, there being but six or so miles between it and the mainland.

11.30. The snowfall now threatens the onset of whiteout conditions with both drift and spray blowing from the crests of the overtaking waves. Ice is now developing over the deck and outside rails. Decks, stanchions, lifeboats, etc. are already well-encrusted.

12 noon. The wind is now registering force 10 – strong gales with winds up to fifty-five miles per hour. Barometer showing 984 millibars and still falling. The motion of the little ship can only be described as violent – 25°+ rolls followed by a sickening pitch at the bow. Bodies and property are hurled indiscriminately and slammed against walls and partitions.
I have found a quiet corner where I can brace my feet against one wall and my back against the other. Fingers clutch at the moulding of the bench back. Am reasonably secure. Try to allow my body to move as if it were part of the vessel.

2 pm. The wind has increased to force 11 – violent storm, near hurricane strength – winds at or greater than seventy-five miles per hour. Beginning to feel physically fatigued. Change to a kneeling position, chest tight against the back of the seat and arms spread-eagled along the moulding.

I look out of the porthole – out and down into the deep green valley of the ocean – the equivalent of a six-storey building. It seems at this moment there can be no more than a foot of water left beneath the keel.

Behind us and bearing down fast is a mountain of sea, sixty feet high or so and towering over the ship, while beneath us is virtually nothing at all. The world is upside down – sea above us, space beneath. With a roar just dimly perceived above the shrieking wind, an avalanche of ocean comes sliding down our back and passes beneath us, without breaking, thank God!

3 pm. No respite: wind now blowing at force 12, nearly 100 miles per hour. Behind us the huge swells continue to climb to the sky and we surge sickeningly forward, due in part to the great push being given by the rising sea and in part to the increase in engine speed required to keep ahead of breaking waves.

So it goes on – hour after hour. We are a mere straw when measured against the power and fury of these seas. It will only end when we can find a harbour into which we can duck for shelter. In the meantime, the ice is making us increasingly top-heavy. It would take only a small navigational error, or a mechanical problem with engines or rudder, for us to be hit on the beam and rolled over like the toy we really are.

4.30 pm. Body aching all over. Limbs losing strength. Torso unwilling to maintain itself in an upright position. It no longer matters to me that I have no control over the situation. One becomes totally fatalistic, emotionally inert, when subjected to such elemental fury. It has been going on so long that I no longer really care – would sell my soul for five minutes of flat water and calm wind.

Yet although we seem to be making little forward headway in these racing seas – hesitating and corkscrewing in the troughs – we are in fact drawing steadily nearer to Cape Adare.

By evening the wind has moderated somewhat – its velocity down to force 7 at about forty miles per hour – but there is little noticeable change in the height of the seas: they simply seem to come down on the ship with less of a rush, less urgency. The blizzarding snow-flurries are dying out, resulting in improved visibility all round. I am much relieved by this, for during the last few hours the watch on the bridge must have been blind more often than not, eyes struggling between the racing crests. Our radar was generally lower than the level of the sea itself, a worrying situation in an area renowned for the accumulation of large and mobile icebergs.

We are now fifteen nautical miles from the tip of Cape Adare. We shall try to seek respite from seas which may take hours to subside, by taking the ship out of the northward flow of the swell. To achieve this, we will turn the point of Cape Adare and enter Robertson Bay – a fifteen-mile-long inlet lying behind the Cape on its western side. There are two serious problems with this. First, the turn westward must be wide and drawn out in order to minimize exposure of the port beam to the direct assault of the following sea. The second is to be found in the Pilot Book for this area:

Robertson Bay should be navigated with great caution. Icebergs are often aground, streams very strong, and winds often violent. Cape Adare (Lat. 78° 18′ S; Long. 170° 15′ E) should be given a wide berth. The bay has a bad reputation, as the current brings in heavy pack with little warning; a vessel should therefore be ready to leave at short notice.

We begin the long westerly swing around the high cliffs of the Cape, and I am amazed at how rapidly the sea calms once we stand in the lee of the Admiralty Range – virtually in the lee of the whole continent of Antarctica. Behind us the huge seas march steadily north along a line extending from the tip of the Adare promontory to New Zealand. Ahead, Robertson Bay seems to be clear of ice, and, as we move southward down it, the 600-foot cliffs of Cape Adare rise menacingly on our left. To starboard, the steep ice and snowbound slopes of the 12,000-foot peaks of the Admiralty Range massif soar, heights which can give rise to a fierce downflow of katabatic winds.

So we begin a long night of sailing up and down the bay. It is too deep to anchor; but it is also necessary to be ready to head quickly for open sea should icebergs or pack ice start accumulating at the mouth of the bay.

The only advantage of the storm has been to bring us into this region so rich in the history of Antarctic exploration. It was here, almost at the tip of Cape Adare, that in 1899 the Norwegian Carsten Borchgrevink was the first to winter-over on the Antarctic continent. Little remains of his hut, although I do briefly catch sight of the cross erected high on the bluff by the grave of Hansen, Borchgrevink's naturalist who died of some untreatable internal complaint.

The site of Borchgrevink's base was also used by Campbell and the men of Scott's Northern Party. They were landed here from *Terra Nova* under difficult sea conditions and erected their winter hut close to that of Borchgrevink's.

The sky darkens earlier in these more northerly regions, and it is a bleak, unwelcoming landscape; half a mile on our left the moraine-like beaches of the southern tip of the peninsula slide past, backed by steeply rising rock slopes showing signs of recent avalanche falls from the high Adare escarpment. Raymond Priestley described this region as a hazardous rookery ground for the thousands of Adélie penguins arriving each spring.

They have great difficulty landing from the sea due to the very heavy northerly swell, as well as the huge chunks of ice which come in with it – frozen missiles – which are hurled around and crush the birds as they try to find their feet. Latecomers, finding no room on the beaches, are compelled to climb the steep slopes to higher ground; Priestley reported finding many dozens of carcasses, the result of crowd-trampling or avalanche.

Further south now, with the last narrow beach left behind, we pass before the face of the Warning Glacier – ice cliffs about fifty feet high topped by a steeply rising, crevassed slope which climbs to the summit of the Cape. The Northern Party encountered heavy ice pressure here where the glacier's advancing front met the ice of the frozen sea: high ridges and deep chasms which were difficult to navigate, together with strong winds and heavy snow. I try to imagine the Robertson Bay they would have known – frozen solid, the constant roar of the winter wind, the sense of being trapped by a ring of mountains which allow no access to the hinterland. In comparison, the bases at Cape Royds and Cape Evans, backed by Erebus and with the expanse of McMurdo Sound spread before them, must have seemed an Antarctic utopia.

Leaving Robertson Bay without mishap the following morning a geologist on the expedition says to me: "Well, we're bloody lucky to get away with it, I'd rather have taken my chances in the open sea. Have you any idea how many rock columns there are in this bay, just beneath the surface? And we could have been completed blocked off in here. Cape Adare's a great gathering place for icebergs, and most of them float around to close off the mouth of the bay."

We are on course for New Zealand, and the end of our trip, but had we taken the ship westward we would have passed Cape Denison and Commonwealth Bay, some 550 miles west of our present position, where Douglas Mawson established his base in January 1912. This was the land he later wrote about as "The Home of the Blizzard" – where the average wind speed for every hour of every day in May was 60.7 mph; where on 15 May the wind averaged 90 mph for twenty-four hours. And it was from these winter quarters that he set out on a fateful journey – the sledging expedition with dogs that was to see the death of his two companions, and his return alone to base: a solitary survival trek that stands alone in the history of polar exploration.

Mawson's expedition to this region had sailed from Hobart, Tasmania,

Iceberg west of Cape Adare. "Cape Adare's a great gathering place for icebergs, and most of them float around to close off the mouth of the bay."

on 2 December 1911. He wished to land three parties along the unexplored coast but only found access to the region in two places. He was able to establish the main base between Commonwealth Bay and Cape Denison, and a subsidiary base on the Shackleton Ice Shelf 1500 miles to the west and southwest. (Frank Wild led the secondary expedition and accomplished an extraordinary coastal survey of the region.) The ship employed was *Aurora*, under its captain John King Davis who, like Douglas Mawson, was a veteran of Shackleton's 1908 *Nimrod* expedition.

In selecting Cape Denison as the site for the main base hut – because access from the sea on a coast beset by ice was good, and because a somewhat gradual ice slope led from there to high terrain – Mawson unwittingly settled in what has sometimes been described as the windiest region of all Antarctica.

On 17 November 1912 Mawson set off with two fellow members of his Australasian Antarctic Expedition, Dr Xavier Mertz and Lieutenant B. E. S. Ninnis. Mertz, a 28-year-old lawyer from Basle, was Switzerland's ski-

*Mawson's hut. "It was from these winter quarters that he set out on a fateful journey –
the sledging expedition with dogs that was to see the death of his two companions, and
his return alone to base: a solitary survival trek that stands alone in the history of polar
exploration."* Photo: Colin Monteath

running champion and a most experienced mountaineer; Ninnis was in
the British Army and had charge of the expedition's dogs. Their intention
was to penetrate the unknown hinterland of high country that lay to the
south and east. Initially the way led over two of the largest – sixty miles
across – and deeply crevassed glaciers in the world, later to be named after
his companions: the treacherously riven Mertz glacier and the "tumultuous
and broken" Ninnis glacier. Early in December a 70-mph blizzard had
them trapped; after three days dogs and sledges had to be dug out, and
deep snow made renewed progress difficult and dangerous. On 14
December they discarded a sledge. Leading the way on skis, Mertz
announced the presence of yet another snow-covered crevasse. Mawson
crossed without difficulty, but then a horrified cry from Mertz spun

Mawson round. There was no one behind him. Ninnis was gone – lost down the apparently bottomless crevasse – and with him his dog team and sledge carrying the tent, most of their equipment, and all the dog food.

All the two men could see in the crevasse was one badly injured dog on a ridge about 150 feet down. They shouted into the abyss for three hours. Nothing. Their ropes would not even reach to the crippled dog.

They were 315 miles from Cape Denison and the hut. For shelter they had a spare tent cover which, draped over skis and sledge struts, made a crude shelter. They still possessed a week's ration for themselves, a cooker and kerosene. Turning for home they began to kill the dogs, starting with the weakest, feeding both themselves and the remaining animals, until the last of them was gone. On Christmas Day they were 160 miles from base. By New Year's Day 1913 Mertz had developed stomach pains and asked to come off the dog meat diet – trying to get by on the few remaining sledging rations. On 6 January Mawson was hauling Mertz on the sledge, even having to put him in his sleeping bag at night. At day's end on 7 January – 100 miles southeast of the hut – Mertz died.

Later Mawson wrote in *The Home of the Blizzard*:

> For hours I lay in my bag, rolling over in my mind all that lay behind and the chance of the future. I seemed to stand alone on the wild shores of the world . . . My physical condition was such that I felt I might collapse at any moment . . . Several of my toes commenced to blacken and fester near the tips and the nails worked loose. There appeared to be little hope . . . It was easy to sleep on in the bag, and the weather was cruel outside.

But the next morning Mawson recovered; he buried Mertz in his sleeping bag, made a rough cross from sledge runners – he had sawed the sledge in half to lessen the load – and set off, with still almost 100 miles to go and virtually no food left.

Fortunately, Mawson possessed an unerring navigational sense – a feeling for time, distance, and direction that enabled him to cross this wasteland, with poor visibility at best, and without a working sledge-meter, an instrument without which distances travelled can only be guessed at.

Daily he was fighting gales which blew him and his now makeshift sledge off course; hauling himself out of crevasses; trying to sleep in the excuse for a tent he had fabricated. And he was alone – all alone – totally isolated in a fastness of ice and shrieking wind on a continent the size of America and Europe combined – no living thing around, neither tree nor bush, not even a mouse. It took him hours to perform even the simplest of tasks – erecting the shelter, lighting the stove, breaking camp. With the soles of his feet falling off, skin and hair sloughing away, he had become a living skeleton when finally helped down the last few hundred feet of the steep ice tongue giving access to the base hut. Normally 210 pounds, he was reduced to less than 100.

Fingers frozen and practically skinless, every movement excruciatingly painful and taking ten times longer than usual, he had sat down to improvise crampons with screws and bits of wood cannibalized from the sledge; he had then fabricated a fifteen-foot rope ladder to attach to the sledge's front end, up which he could climb when he fell into a crevasse – if the sledge held in the deep snow of its lip, that is. Crossing the glacier named after Mertz on the penultimate leg of this terrible journey, Mawson fell twice to dangle at the end of a single harness rope in deep fissures, managing on both occasions to climb his ladder to where he could "hurl himself up and over the rim" (*hurl* himself . . . how on earth did he manage that?) to lie semiconscious in the snow. He would undoubtedly have slipped or been blown off the steep downhill glacier slopes without his homemade crampons, yet he had to suffer the pain of the screw-heads slowly being pushed up through the wood to penetrate his feet – feet from which the soles had separated, having to be bloodily and constantly re-attached, held in place, with improvised bindings.

There's a sad twist to this story – the irony of history's timing. Mertz might have survived if Mawson had known what is now understood about vitamin A. After Ninnis's death and the loss of provisions, Mawson killed the dogs and rationed out the sinewy meat of the starved animals. But it was the dogs' livers that he – together with the other explorers of his time – knew contained the vitamin A essential for survival. So he daily cooked the required portion – it gave no fat, was simply charred on the outside, remained raw within – and he insisted that they eat their portion, although he found the taste "repellent". Poor Mertz had to be strongly persuaded to swallow his portion of dog liver, as it seems that some intuitive sense hinted that the stuff was killing him. Yet it was not until 1968 that research opened up the possibility that acute vitamin A toxicity – Hypervitaminosis

A – might have been responsible for Mertz's death; and not until 1971 was it discovered that the Greenland husky – the dogs used on Mawson's expedition – secretes higher levels of vitamin A in its liver than any other dog: ten toxic doses for the average human adult in a single husky liver.

Douglas (later Sir Douglas) Mawson was the last of the great explorers of the Heroic Age. His journey was in the tradition of Scott, Amundsen and Shackleton, yet he is not part of the European polar experience. Although he was born in England, Mawson belongs to Australia where he is revered but his story, like so much of Australian history, seems little known above the Tropic of Capricorn.

It is tempting for people who have an interest in Antarctic exploration to argue who was the greatest of the heroes. It is, of course, comparing apples to oranges to plums. Partisans of Scott, for example, will dismiss Shackleton as a mere adventurer and Amundsen as, perhaps worse, a professional who made it all seem too easy. Supporters of the other side will point to Scott's blunders, errors in judgment, flaws in personality. It is silly, of course. Few of us who, in hindsight, debate these issues could have accomplished a fraction of what any of them did. But we are, nevertheless, entitled to our opinions and, in mine, Douglas Mawson must finally be given the laurels.

If his ordeal is to be compared with that of anyone else, it would naturally be with Shackleton, constantly improvising in the face of disaster, journeying enormous distances in the shadow of almost certain death. But Shackleton had one great advantage over Mawson; he had the companionship, from beginning to end, of faithful and able men. Not one of them died – there were no ghosts to haunt him on that incredible journey from Elephant Island to South Georgia.

Mawson, however, suffered not only physically, sustaining damage that remained with him, in some degree, for the rest of his life, but he endured it and bore entirely alone the memory of the men who were lost. It is impossible to imagine his overwhelming loneliness, the sense of being, for all intents and purposes, the only human being on the face of the earth.

In the drama of Mawson, more than any other, lies the metaphor for Antarctica. This wild continent is far more than a land of severe and capricious weather – many places are that. But there is no other place on earth that is as isolated by virtue of its climate and the fierce ocean that surrounds it. No other place is as removed from the life of the world, is as

Maritime East Antarctic. "No other place is as removed from the life of the world, is as cut off from the normal expectations of our human existence …"

cut off from the normal expectations of our human existence as this one. Even now, with the proliferation of bases and the great increase in tourism, the continent stands apart. Humanity has just barely made its mark on the outer edge. The rest remains as it has always been – lonely, hostile, inaccessible – pure and white and impossibly beautiful.

PART TWO

EAST ANTARCTICA: THE "FAR SIDE"

7

SUBANTARCTIC
SURVIVORS

THE TOUGH BIRDS AND BEASTS OF CROZET AND KERGUELEN

The grand sweep of the continent west of Cape Adare to the Weddell Sea runs into the full fury of the circumpolar winds which flow down over East Antarctica (the "Far Side") from the polar uplands, where the thickness of ice reaches several thousand feet – northerly and westerly winds which militate against the kind of summer window found in West Antarctica. Because its climate is so severe, and the distance from any point of departure – be it from South America, New Zealand, South Africa, or Australia – is so great, the human presence in East Antarctica is slight, and the history of exploration here is not as rich as that carried out in West Antarctica.

True, Kerguelen Island was visited once by the redoubtable Captain Cook. There, on a miserable Christmas Eve in 1776, he named a small, exposed harbour Port Christmas in honour of the occasion. Today these islands are in the possession of France which maintains two small but civilized bases. And there is a truly tiny meteorological station on Heard Island manned by less than a handful of Australians.

On the continent itself there is even less activity. The Australians have a few bases, as do the Russians. The Chinese, latecomers to the scene, have a rather squalid base in an exquisite setting, complete with Christmas decorations in the dining room and a statue of Sun-Yat-Sen, the Father of the Revolution, in the parlour. Compared to the semi-urban sprawl of McMurdo and the concentration of bases in the Peninsula, the scientific population is puny indeed, and only the two Australian bases are touched by any sense of history: they are named after their hero, Mawson, and his ship's captain, Davis.

Mawson represents a natural link between the East and West sides of the continent. He played a key role in Shackleton's 1908 expedition, and his own great trek of 1912 is essentially part of the western Antarctic

111

history. But in the years between 1929 and 1931 he returned to the continent to explore by sea the coast of East Antarctica, making the two voyages of a combined British, Australian and New Zealand Antarctic Research Expedition, known as Mawson's B.A.N.Z.A.R.E. voyages. By 1928 the advance of Norwegian exploration – and to lesser degree the influence of the French presence – on the "Far Side" was causing some anxiety in Britain, and the goal of Sir Douglas's two expeditions was as much to counter Norwegian ambition and claim territory for the Commonwealth, as it was to enhance geographic and scientific knowledge.

The Commonwealth and Britain together paid for the hire and refit of Scott's expedition ship *Discovery* – a well founded and ice-worthy vessel built for Scott's first expedition of 1902–3. John King Davis – who had been the master of *Aurora* on Mawson's 1911–13 expedition was the captain of *Discovery*'s first B.A.N.Z.A.R.E. expedition. It is interesting to note that Mawson considered the "Heroic Era" of Antarctic exploration to have ended with Shackleton's death in South Georgia after the First World War; and that the "Mechanical Era" began with the introduction of technology – aeroplanes and tractor sledges. Mawson used a seaplane for land reconnaissance on the *Discovery* voyages. As a result of the *Discovery* expeditions Princess Elizabeth Land and MacRobertson Land became, in 1932, part of the Australian Antarctic Territory.

In the course of these journeys Mawson made a number of observations. He spoke of the terrible seas around the Kerguelen Archipelago, and most especially in the vicinity of Heard Island. Small boat landings were both dangerous and difficult. The frequent and rapid changes in weather, even in early summer – with gale force winds – force 8 and up – an unpredictable and almost daily occurrence. Finally, he was consistently threatened by the shifting pack in which leads were scarce and which, without warning, could close up with ice to trap his ship and diminish what limited time they had.

More recently a band of anonymous Russians undertook long and arduous treks to the interior across the virtually unexplored ice sheet. In 1956–7 and again in the following year they left the coastal base of Mirny* near the West Ice Shelf to traverse the 12,000-foot-high plateau – a pioneering journey during which they were short on oxygen and subjected

* For East Antarctica see map on page 58.

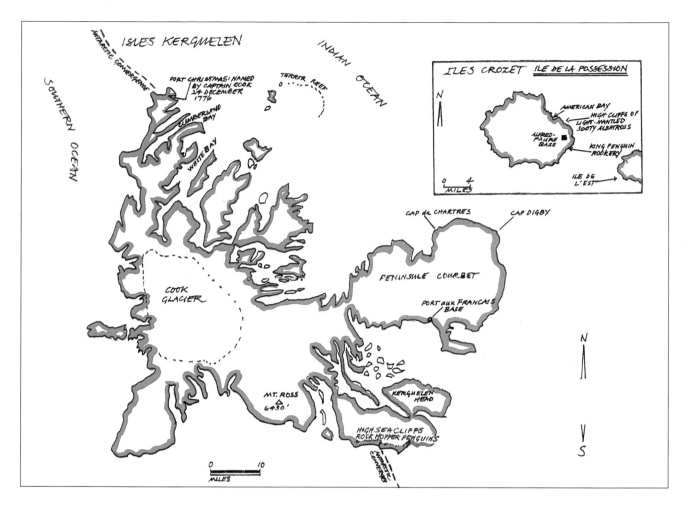

Isles of Kerguelen (Inset: Ile de la Possession, Crozet Group)

to the lowest temperatures on earth. Finally, deep in the interior, they reached their goal – the most far away position from any point on the coastline. Here, at a distance of some 1250 miles from Mirny, they established a scientific station called, appropriately, the Pole of Inaccessibility. Then they established Vostok base, the coldest-known place on the globe where temperatures of –80°F are almost routinely recorded.

Any real appreciation of their accomplishments must come from seeing with one's own eyes the formidable coastline which fringed the interior wilderness of ice with which they had to contend. There is nothing here but an iced sea and the swelling iced dome of land – space without end, a horizon that recedes with every step. There just is sky and ice swept up into horizontal vistas of incomprehensible magnitude. What meagre "right of presence" man has here is but barely supportable. East Antarctica still belongs, and rightfully, almost entirely to the animals who come to breed –

the seals, petrels, skuas and, perhaps most of all, to the emperor penguins, whose breeding grounds are limited to the remote stretches of coastline that harbour perpetual ice.

Grey, rain-spitting clouds attend our departure from South Africa on a late November evening. Our ship – a Russian icebreaker. Our destination – Les Iles Crozet, France's Subantarctic possessions in the South Indian Ocean: a small group of desolate islands sitting precisely in the middle of the Roaring Forties – fifteen hundred or so miles south and slightly east of the Cape of Good Hope. Our route is to stay very close to that taken by Mawson on his first *Discovery* voyage.

The passage, which should have taken four or five days, takes close to seven. The weather is filthy – full-blown gales for a week – and the round bottom of the icebreaker, together with lack of stabilizers, causes it to roll far more than any ship with a keel. In an attempt to ease my rising anxiety, the captain has assured me that the ship has been designed to roll up to 80°. I am not convinced; already we have rolled through 55°, trembling uncertainly over the water until suddenly snapping back. Another 25° is simply inconceivable, yet the westerly winds continue to bedevil us, rolling the high swells constantly on to our beam – winds which will inevitably make helicopter flying over Crozet difficult for a pilot.

Knowing this, it is with some diffidence that we climb into the ship's helicopter together with a couple of Australian scientists. The windshield is patched with Scotch tape; the fuselage and rotors are freshly painted with cheap, green paint which comes off at a touch. There is no way to lessen the din of the huge rotor-airfoils tearing at the inner ear as the engine rises to crescendo pitch for lift-off. Slowly we spiral upward before the pilot points the thing in the direction he wants to go and accelerates away, tail-rotor up, nose nervously peering down surveying the terrain. As the helicopter closes in on the barren slopes of the coastal hills it rises a thousand feet or more, following the contours of the ground below, before lurching forward – like some short-sighted stick insect – towards the next high ridge. It slides upward again and the sea on the far side of the island comes into view.

The land below is desolate: outcrops of black volcanic rock surrounded by clumps of short tussock grass, small ravines running in series and walled in by steep craggy slopes, and areas of bog where dark water glistens. It will be treacherous walking: and there are few landmarks to help fix a position. But it is a short run – three miles only – before we descend over the roofs of the long rectangular buildings comprising the scientific station and come to rest on the small ill-defined helicopter pad. Surveying us quizzically as they lean against the wall of their Headquarters hut, cigarette smoke from the odd Gauloise blowing away around their heads, stands a group of bearded base personnel taking the air – men who have committed themselves to stay for twelve months or longer in this remote and lonely spot in the Southern Ocean.

Politely, and I hope, respectfully, we acknowledge their presence, then trail out over the sparse grass of a headland which slopes gradually down towards the sea. Below the rim of the escarpment, 90,000 king penguins and their chicks spread like an occupying army at the head of a broad inlet. The young penguin chicks stand stiffly, heads erect, seemingly oblivious to the procession of adult birds moving to and fro – some outward-bound to fish, others returning to regurgitate their catch to their young. I think – not for the first time – how remarkable it is that after an often lengthy absence at sea a returning parent is able to move unerringly to find its own offspring among these thousands of other birds.

Gentle and seductive cadences rise and fall, a chorus of musical, throaty whisperings. The birds perform like a huge choir singing part-song, the refrain being initiated by one group somewhere in the colony, taken up by another cluster at a further remove, then by another, and another, until some sense of communal harmony seems to be satisfied. Then this homophonic part-singing will die away, only to start again in a different part of the rookery. If I were to compose the song of Circe which enchanted Odysseus and his sailors, I would build it on a single motif – that of the penguins' enticing and lilting whirrings.

In contrast to penguin rookeries in West Antarctica – on the Peninsula and offshore islands, for example – these in East Antarctica seem to be less pungent, less noticeably a quagmire of slippery guano. Perhaps the difference in summer temperatures between the two coasts accounts for this. Western regions are sometimes referred to as the "banana belt" because the summers can be relatively warm – a warmth which melts the snow and ice, turning guano into an oozy, slick substance resembling a ripe, dissolving Camembert. But the sun is seen less frequently in the east, and its warmth is diminished: hence, even on mudflat and tussock grass, accumulated droppings tend to break down less and remain relatively firm and odourless.

King penguins – mother and child. "The young penguin chicks stand stiffly, heads erect, seemingly oblivious to the procession of adult birds moving to and fro ..."

The king penguin at three feet is almost a foot shorter than the emperor – the largest of the Antarctic penguins – but the adults of both species share the same brilliant black, orange-pink, and white markings. Young king chicks, however, are drab in comparison with young emperors, their juvenile plumage a dense "woolly" mat of brown hair which moults away piecemeal after about six months, leaving the new young adult with its full complement of colourful sea-going feathers. Young emperors, on the other hand, start their life in a soft blue-grey downy coat, which makes them very beautiful indeed, right from the start.

King penguins – like those I am now observing – breed and live year

King penguins – convention delegates. "The mature birds take little notice of our presence, moving purposefully on their single-minded peregrinations, stumbling over the feet of anyone in their path, apparently quite undeterred by such large 'penguins' in their midst."

round in the vicinity of subantarctic islands. It is not a bird of Polar latitudes like the emperor which breeds in the depth of winter on the sea ice. Given that the habitat of kings is the grass flats of more temperate islands – providing a background of soft browns and greens – the shaggy brown fluff of the chicks allows them to blend naturally into the landscape. Similarly, the young emperor in its pale-grey coat is a child of the ice and snow. Thus, before they moult into the chromatically brilliant feathers of adulthood, when the sea finally beckons, the vulnerable youngsters of both species are camouflaged for life on land. The almost identical colouring of the adults is that of every other penguin – dark on top, light below – an adaptation for life in the sea. This pattern, which is repeated throughout the marine environment – for diving birds, seals, even killer whales – makes the animal difficult to spot from above and equally difficult from below against the light.

The sun comes out as I wander around the fringes of the rookery, transforming the scene into a shimmering kaleidoscope of reflected light emanating from the plumage of the adult penguins. The French scientist who accompanies me smiles. "Look at that," he says. "You know, we don't see the sun for more than six days in the year. You're lucky!"

The mature birds take little notice of our presence, moving purposefully on their single-minded peregrinations, stumbling over the feet of anyone in their path, apparently quite undeterred by such large "penguins" in their midst. In contrast, however, many chicks are quite curious about us: they approach to within less than a yard and look up at us, shoulders hunched, head slightly to one side, film-like membrane sliding up and over the eye like the slow-moving shutter over the lens of a camera, and just stare. They seem to display a genuinely intelligent interest in our arrival, aware of us as things newly arrived in their environment, and exhibit all the characteristics of inquisitiveness. Although some are bolder than others in satisfying their curiosity, it appears to me that their behaviour in general could well be the response to an innate spirit of inquiry, indulged in for its own sake.

A tidal pool marks the southern extremity of the rookery, and here many young elephant seals are exhibiting what appears to be playful "submarine" tactics, swimming close to the surface then bringing only nose and eyes above the water to take a look at what is going on. They sometimes remain stationary in this position for several minutes, fixing one with an inscrutable gaze – while on the beach others of their kind lie around slothfully undergoing their own moult, old skin peeling off them like rotten wallpaper on a damp wall. In close confrontations the younger pups roll their eyes, yet still allow you to stand alongside – an intimacy which provokes nothing more aggressive than the odd belch: a propulsion of air through the tubes of great sonority, yet rounded off with a

OPPOSITE: *The king inquisitor. "… their behaviour in general could well be the response to an innate spirit of inquiry, indulged in for its own sake."*

superhuman hiss and gasp as pressure is released. They seem to like doing it, eyes conveying a certain sense of relief at such a thorough exercising of the exhaust systems. And a belch from one encourages a similar retort from another: a communication of sorts?

Provocative creatures: awkward slobs of blubber as they heave themselves laboriously around on land; yet streamlined torpedoes as they scythe submerged through the water.

How many walks does one remember – sorties across country that linger in the mind as remarkable, surreal events? Well, this afternoon hike across the island is in that category because the terrain is the wildest and most elemental over which I have ever ventured, and because at the end we hope to see one of the most beautiful birds in the world. The brief sun of early morning has disappeared. A low ceiling of overall grey cloud cover sets in as we leave the Base Headquarters. We are walking across the northeast corner of the island to the high cliffs where light-mantled sooty albatrosses are nesting. It is hard going: the ground is spongy (it is possible to lose half a leg from time to time in a black peat-like hole), the grass generally confined to hummocks, yet both rock and thin topsoil are overspread by a great variety of delicately formed lichen and flora – fragile growth which we must avoid trampling insofar as it is possible. In between are stretches of crumbly volcanic rock and scree, deceptively unstable and slithery underfoot. Rain threatens, but, save for a brief sprinkle, never materializes.

The terrain slopes slightly uphill and it is difficult to gauge just how far away is the line of sky that marks where the land drops away to the ocean. I look back after about half an hour and realize that the high wireless masts of the base have disappeared. I wonder how we'll find our way back if the weather clamps down. It is a featureless landscape with no distinctive landmarks left or right; ahead, more of the same except for the broad band of sky which at least defines our destination – a drop of several hundred feet to the sea where, on ledges and in crevices, the nesting birds are to be found.

Now the land begins to slope seaward and is becoming noticeably more swampy, clearly a drainage area for surface water which, given the frequency of rainfall, is in a constant state of run-off. We stop for a breather, leaning against a convenient tall rock at the end of the stone ridge we are following. The fell rises abruptly behind, practically obscuring the sky. I had no idea while descending that the slope would be so steep, and have not a clue as to where on the skyline we have come from in order to strike this ridge.

The French guide suddenly announces that we are now dropping down to the sea – that we should walk more cautiously from this point on as rifts in the ground are frequent and often hidden until one is right on top of them – and that once we reach the base of the stone ridge we should follow it where it runs downhill toward the cliffs.

From then on the terrain falls away even more sharply – green, tussocky, and treacherous with sink holes – and then there is nothing but space. The abrupt cessation of the land comes as a psychological rather than a physical shock.

I look left and right to find something substantial within my field of vision, and the vertical face of a flanking bluff comes slowly into focus. Only when I am able to scan its rock wall down to the sea, before returning to look out on the openness of the scene immediately before me, does some sense of my own stability – firmly anchored, feet to ground – return (the sudden thought of "nothingness" has perceptions reeling for a moment). Now the horizontal line signifying the limits of the land firms up; and the void becomes normally perceptible as the old familiar sky.

I give myself a couple of minutes to look around and assess the angle of the slope. The final hundred feet of slope are carpeted with a mossy vegetation which wraps the brim of the cliff in soft, blanket-like folds completely disguising the sharp edge of the drop. The terrain is not without hazard: soggy crevasses lurk unsuspectingly in green ground, rendering every step a potential disaster. To both left and right along the whole rim of the precipice skeins of water – sometimes lost to sight beneath the vegetation – come together to form small rivulets, find common outlets, and cascade in fine-spun waterfalls to the far-away ocean below.

Somewhere – close to the edge of the land, in the grass or beneath an overhanging bank or rock ledge affording protection from rain or falling debris – are the nests of the birds I have come to see. They are on the windward side of the island where the westerlies will provide immediate lift for take-off.

The light-mantled sooty is a relatively small albatross when compared to

The light-mantled sooty. "… a nearly perfect avian creation – a superb flying machine that is also a sheer delight to the eye."

the wanderer or royal albatross. Yet what it lacks in size it more than makes up for in appearance, especially when seen on the nest with its wings folded, its long legs and large feet tucked away beneath its tail. From any angle it is a wonderful blending of clean and elegantly proportioned ovoid forms, each flowing rhythmically and effortlessly into the other, sensuously smooth, exquisitely coloured and evoking the strongest of aesthetic emotions.

From an artistic point of view, the light-mantled sooty is a nearly perfect avian creation – a superb flying machine that is also a sheer delight to the eye. When in repose, nothing disturbs the harmony achieved by the volumetric flow of part to part. Even the line of the large and powerful bill is in flowing counterpoint to the curvature of head and breast, a rapier when seen head-on, yet clearly revealing its function as tubular and fluted naves when in profile. The colouration is restrained, each hue perfectly modulated to the next, while at the same time sharply defining the particular volume beneath it: the white breast; the charcoal-grey mantled head reflecting brown highlights; wings and tail feathers grey to grey-blue with a touch of brown on the underside; a final touch of blue accentuating the tip of the bill.

But it is the eyes – dark brown in a dusky head, which would be all but lost were it not for the lustrous encircling ring of white – which represent the greatest beauty of this bird. These white rings are one of nature's brilliant, painterly touches: highly visible accents which not only enliven this delicate and subdued colour scheme, but also give to the eyes – especially when seen head-on – a penetration, almost fierceness, as well as a look of inquisitive intelligence. As we stare at it, the bird, like the penguins, seems utterly unfazed by our presence.

This smaller albatross is less dependent than the large wanderer on the planing technique of flying, on using air currents to maintain stability and direction. Both the sooty albatross and the light-mantled sooty have smaller, lighter bodies than other members of the family, yet still maintain the long wings required for a more heavily bodied bird. This lower body-mass ratio to wing surface gives them a positive aerial advantage: they are able to fly more in the manner of a "powered" aircraft, as opposed to that of a glider – propelling themselves when the wind isn't there to do it for them, thus having at their command more flying options and a greater range of deftness and manoeuvrability when on the wing. The following extract from Louis J. Halle's wonderful book, *The Sea and the Ice*, describes the situation perfectly:

> The great albatrosses . . . as distinct from the two sooties, are massive birds that depend on the momentum of their mass in a high wind – momentum being the product of mass and velocity. Living as they do in unobstructed space, they have little occasion for tight manoeuvers or sudden stops. According to those who have witnessed it, when they land on their nesting grounds, which they can do only in flat open areas, they have difficulty reducing their speed enough, so that the wanderers sometimes tip up on their noses and tumble over before coming to a stop. To take the air again they generally have to launch themselves from a height and into a wind. The two sooty albatrosses, by contrast, are notable for their deftness on the wing, which they have sometimes demonstrated by landing on the tip of a ship's mast. The lightness of their bodies, relative to the size

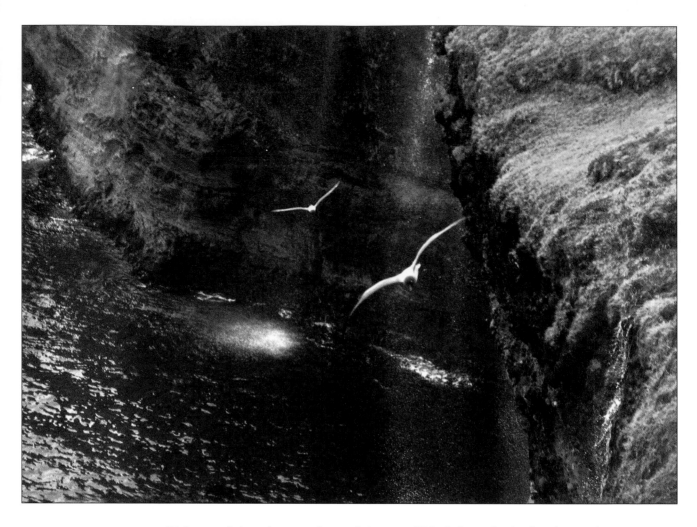

Light-mantled sooties returning to their nests. "I look down for the first time to the waters of the South Indian Ocean some four hundred feet below, as the sooties swoop in, hugging the cliff face."

of their wings, and, above all, their long, cuneate tails, enable them to land gently enough on the ledges of their nesting cliffs. A great albatross, trying to land at the nesting site of a light-mantled sooty, would surely be wrecked.

As Patricia and I edge nervously downhill a flight of sooties comes into view. On my right, the steep face of the precipice cuts inland for a hundred yards or so before turning to swing back out to sea, forming a deep cleft – into which I can now peer. Through an almost imperceptible screen of mist created by the line of spidery waterfalls, I look down for the first time to the waters of the South Indian Ocean some four hundred feet below, as the sooties swoop in, hugging the cliff face.

There they are, four birds flying in a line all at the same height, midway between sea and cliff top where the air would likely be more turbulent. Their narrow wings are fully extended, their flight posture seemingly unaffected by either updraft or downdraft– a distance that is unswervingly maintained, until, one after the other, they use their long pointed tails like an aircraft's elevators to send them soaring upward for a pinpoint landing on the narrow upland ridges where their nests are placed

Their feet come out from under the tail to dangle and act as airbrakes, while the angle of the wing tips is narrowed to spill the air, reduce approach speed. They settle easily where they want. This ability of the sooties to fly under their own power – with the minimum of wind assistance – is the factor which allows them to venture further south than their larger relatives, to venture into and beyond the frontier where open sea meets heavy pack ice. There the oppressive weight of the ice, and the lightness of the easterly winds, produce a region of relatively calm water. They need neither strong winds, nor a heavy swell and the large waves which provide updraft, to remain effectively airborne. Because of their ability to make this southerly sweep – even as far as the Antarctic coast – the light-mantled sooties can follow the ice edge all the way around the continent.

Like encounters on West Antarctica's Deception Island, these moments of intimacy with wild creatures are the more surprising when you consider the mass slaughter of penguins and seals carried out on these islands as recently as sixty years ago – the men of the sealing ships cruelly and stupidly bludgeoning every living animal to death, even suckling pups, thereby ensuring that there could be no future harvests.

On Crozet – Mawson's first stop on his 1929–30 expedition to East Antarctica – he saw the sealers at their work on these very beaches. On 2 November 1929 he recorded: "Very great numbers sea-elephants along the shore – all being slaughtered by 'Kilfinora' men. The bulls, cows and young down to about 3 months old slain for blubber. The suckling young merely hit on head with maul and left." On 3 November he wrote "The 'Kilfinora' returned early in the morning. Their men have been continuing all day with the slaughter of elephants."

Professor Harvey Johnston, a biologist on Mawson's expedition wrote as follows in his own journal for 3 November: "The latter [the sealers] anchored during the night at another part of the island (Ship's Cove) but came back early this morning and a party was on the island before us. We saw them shooting the animals at very close range (bulls and cows) and knocking all the seal pups on the head with a sledgehammer. Not a solitary animal was left in the harems which they visited, and I was informed that the men would be there for another two days to clean the place up. I assumed that they meant to dispose of the carcasses of the slaughtered animals, but they meant to take every seal there; a dreadful massacre that is disgraceful since it means practically wiping out the entire herds that congregate there to breed. The ship had come from other islands where they had acted similarly. The sealing business is a sickening, senseless butchery . . . Only the blubber is sliced off, the rest of each animal being left for the skuas and giant petrels. One could see these scavengers (skuas) tearing out the eyes and the intestines and dancing and squabbling with yards of small intestines dragged out in various directions from the beast, while the beach was soaked in blood.'

The history of sealing in the South Atlantic commenced as early as the mid-eighteenth century following Captain James Cook's discovery of South Georgia, and his report on the size of the fur seal and elephant seal populations there. Some estimates have it that fur seals were rare in South Georgia by the 1820s. Similarly, six years after the discovery by Europeans of Antarctica in 1819, the population of Antarctic fur seals in West Antarctica's South Shetland Islands was also almost extinct. The fur seal's commercial value lay in its skin which was made into leather coats, whereas the elephant seal was killed for the oil derived from its blubber, one seal providing up to two barrels. In a Europe becoming increasingly industrialized oil was a booming commodity. And after West Antarctica the seal colonies of Crozet and the Kerguelen Archipelago on the "Far Side" suffered a similar plundering.

There are albatrosses on our first morning at Kerguelen, some 700 nautical miles east of Crozet – sooties, heralding the day which is windy and cold, but dry.

Kerguelen was discovered by a Frenchman, Yves Joseph de Kerguelen-Tremerac in 1772. Douglas Mawson was greatly impressed by this "wonderful island" when *Discovery* arrived there on 12 November 1929. His captain was less impressed. It was snowing, and the extract from Captain Davis's log reads: " ... at 6.25 sighted land through the snow, which was the high cliff just west of Cape Digby ... a risky business, as if

Macaroni rookery, Kerguelen Island. "The vast colony of macaroni penguins …
stretches almost to the horizon."

the wind had gone into east … we should have difficulty in keeping off the
shore."

The Kerguelen beaches of Cap de Chartres and Cap Digby are home
to an astonishing collection of flying birds, swimming birds and seals – all
going about their business with apparent unconcern for their neighbour,
whatever sort of animal that happens to be. It makes little difference from
where one surveys the scene – either from the higher levels of soggy grass
and tussock above the beaches, or down among the throng on the beach
itself – the place is so humming with life that drama and vignettes of
animal behaviour are literally at one's feet. The vast colony of macaroni
penguins at Cap de Chartres – birds somewhat smaller than the Adélie
and crested with long orange-yellow plumes arcing from the forehead –
stretches almost to the horizon. They are a restless lot, the adults moving
as penguins do back and forth to the water, chicks quivering expectantly
for food, while platoons of birds march in pairs or straggly long lines up
and down well-worn trails on the rookery's upland perimeter.

The skuas are marauding, overflying the colony at low-level, spotting for

unguarded penguin eggs – often successfully. Manoeuvring like a hawk, one of these powerful flyers arrests itself in mid-flight, wings spiralling above its back like helicopter blades, to land on target, breaking the shell of an egg then and there, and devouring the embryo. The reaction of the penguins is nonchalant enough: they shuffle aside to give the skua room – look the other way, so to speak. But when two skuas, operating as a team, descend to take out a weak or sickly chick, consternation breaks out on the ground – whirrings and hissings from many penguin throats and attempts to deter the invaders, before they touch down, by an upward stabbing of beaks and a turbulent whacking of powerful and dangerous flippers. But it is early in the summer when we arrive at Kerguelen – egg time only: very few chicks as yet to be picked off.

It is only on Kerguelen that the northern giant petrel becomes a near Antarctic breeder, more commonly nesting in other subantarctic regions to the north. Several of them circle the macaroni colony in company with the skuas, but while the skuas criss-cross the penguin colony diagonally, the petrels – larger birds altogether – hug the perimeter, flying round and round with little deviation in either height or heading. I don't change my position on the cliff and they don't change theirs: every few minutes one glides past at eye level, no more than two feet from my nose, tail spread, wings quite still save for the flickering movement of independent wing-tip feathers, acknowledging one's presence only by the briefest of glances. In comparing them to skuas and other species of petrels, the anatomical lines of the giant petrel remind one more of the unwieldy bulk of a military transport plane, rather than the sleek, tube-like fuselage of the commercial airliner. I am surprised that with their box-like airframe and preponderant beak they fly so effortlessly and gracefully. Certainly on the ground they are positively ungainly, even unstable, lurching from side to side with wings upraised for balance, long graceless legs spread wide to support their disproportionate, archetypal, ugly duckling appearance.

As they wheel round and round the macaroni rookery, I think how baleful they look, funereal and vulture-like. Like the scavengers they are, they circle endlessly. The mottled monochromatic black-brown-grey of their colouring is relieved only by the pinkish yellow ochre of a heavy and

OPPOSITE: *Macaroni Penguins going for a walk. "…platoons of birds march in pairs or straggly long lines up and down well-worn trails on the rookery's upland perimeter."*

disproportionate bill – as the drab colouring of the vulture is broken by the harsh red of their naked heads. The bill of the giant petrel is quite incredible – two-tiered, with tubular nostrils superimposed for excess salt excretion. The whole aspect gives them the look of a flying undertaker.

Giant petrels feed at sea, guzzling krill, fish, and squid (and sometimes smaller birds); yet they are also effective land scavengers, able to rip open the carcasses of seals or penguins with their powerful beaks. They seem to be on scavenging patrol as they circle the outer edge of the rookery, for it is perhaps more likely that a fallen penguin, rabbit* or bird will be spotted on the open ground surrounding the rookery, than in the midst of these thousands of birds.

Indeed, the fringes of the vegetation where I stand overlooking the macaronis is a graveyard – a grim reminder of Antarctic mortality, littered with whitening bones and skulls: as if creatures *in extremis* have taken to the heath to die, away from the living sea. No doubt the giant petrels know exactly what they are doing in making their endless sweeps around the colony's ever-shifting outer edge.

Walking away from the rookery along the twisting line of lichen-covered rocks and boulders that marks the boundary between beach and upland heath, we suddenly spot a giant petrel chick sitting alone atop an untidy nest of small stones and general debris, on open ground, in a most exposed position. About five or six weeks old – a grey-white fluffball about a foot tall, sitting absolutely upright, neck extended, with the sharply projecting bill that already looks ill-fitting as if stolen from some other species.

It sits imperiously, like a reigning princeling, no more than three feet away, looking me straight in the eye. I crouch down to appear less intimidating, to obtain a closer, more intimate view. Reassured, the bird starts to preen itself. Then stopping after a couple of minutes, it turns its eyes front again, and stares at me unblinkingly. It opens and shuts its bill several times – closes its eyes and seems to go to sleep looking very much like a soft, fluffy toy. There are no clues here – save for the beak – to suggest the dark ponderous adult into which this appealing youngster will grow. (I'm told that some individuals which are born in these far southern latitudes remain pale or quite white throughout their entire adulthood – more ghostly, but less funereal.)

---

* Rabbits were introduced to several subantarctic islands, with disastrous impact on the local ecology, as in Australia.

130

Giant petrel chick. "It sits imperiously, like a reigning princeling, no more than three feet away, looking me straight in the eye."

The parents of my companion must be away feeding. But, although it may appear to be helpless and alone, this young bird is quite capable of defending itself. Predators are quickly discouraged by the chick's ability to regurgitate a foul-smelling stream of stomach contents, more than likely half-digested, rotting fish mixed with strong digestive juices. If it happens to you, the smell can never be removed from your clothes. Without further ado, they must be consigned to the dustbin.

A constant light wind is blowing in from the sea across the nest, ruffling the young bird's delicate feathers, and I realize that this is the reason for choosing such an exposed nesting site: a wind-assisted take-off allows the heavy adult bird to become airborne quickly, with a minimum expenditure of energy as it leaves the chick to search for more food.

The petrel sleeps on and I slowly pull myself upright and stare out over the boulder-covered beach. A full minute passes before I am able to separate living things from rocks. Although the whole foreground is littered with seals – elephant seals predominating, together with a few visiting fur seals – none of these creatures can be immediately perceived. Only just coming into focus – no more than twenty feet before me – is an enormous bull elephant seal. In fact, had he not pulled his head up to yawn and thus expose a huge red cavity of mouth, he might well have remained invisible – simply appearing as a large elliptical boulder with a surface of variegated greys and browns. In all, there must be fifty or more – hitherto unnoticed within my field of vision.

I feel very much the odd man out in a place where the dramas of this animal world are unaffected in any way by the existence of human beings. Every creature here performs its function in a completely natural environment, free from questions of right or wrong, or notions of an individual destiny. Turning to survey the whole scene, I see that the summits of the low hills to the south and west are dusted with a light fall of new snow; on the drab-green uplands pairs of wandering albatrosses are performing the first steps of their mating dance, bobbing and weaving before each other in a desultory fashion, then relapsing into normal behaviour and sitting comfortably side by side until the next round of excitement has them on their feet. Off to my right the skuas are still overflying the rookery; the macaronis are guarding, feeding, or marching to and from the higher ground; the petrels circle; seals stretch, yawn and belch. . . .

Now it is afternoon. A cold wind is gusting up to 35 mph as the Russian helicopter pilot inches us to earth at Cape Digby, feeling his way down through the constantly shifting currents of air. A quarter-mile walk over thin grass leads a long strip of beach – extensive areas of small boulders and pebbles broken by stretches of sand, and shallow sink-holes filled with oozy grey mud.

Unlike the boulder-covered foreshore at Cap de Chartres of the morning – where the bodies of the seals are indistinguishable from the rounded forms of the large rocks – there is no camouflage possible here. The boulder-free openness and relative narrowness of the beach, with the sea clearly marking its limits, ensures that everybody is highly visible. I have the impression that I am watching a teeming natural circus of performing animals – each creature a solo act in its own private ring.

Elephant seals are everywhere. On the high ground to the north the larger adult bulls dominate the scene, bellowing their claims for both territory and females. Several pairs of these mature bulls – each of which could measure

Elephant seal guarding harem. "… the larger adult bulls dominate the scene, bellowing their claims for both territory and females."

eighteen feet in length and weigh up to three tons or more – are engaged in struggles for dominance. They rear up face to face, their huge jaws splayed open to expose huge mouths armed with tusk-like incisors. Each male parries its opponent's thrust, feints on its own account, then lunges at the other's neck or flank, either to rip the skin and do real damage or to simply make superficial contact and warn the rival off. They roar loudly and continuously, sound emanating from the large inflatable nostrils which serve as resonating chambers and drop trunk-like over the mouth – hence the name "elephant seal". I watch this heavy breathing, eyeball-to-eyeball encounter, and find myself wondering if rankness of breath might possibly influence the outcome: there are moments, standing downwind when it would seem to be the most important repellent in the animal's armoury. After a suitable display of aggression the warriors subside, retiring to their corners, as it were, before the next round gets underway. But although much of the encounter is sound and fury, their skirmishes are serious and much blood is spilled in the course of an afternoon.

The beach supports two penguin rookeries: one of the big orange, black-and-white kings; the other of smaller black-and-white gentoos. Already the first gentoo chicks of the season are out and about, yet I see no sign of skuas overflying the rookery – in marked contrast to the skua activity over the macaroni colony at Cap de Chartres where few youngsters were to be seen. If there are territorial boundaries between the rookeries, they are not observed; the smaller black-and-white gentoos wobble nonchalantly between the tall, colourful kings – neither species deigning to acknowledge the presence of the other.

By subantarctic standards it is a perfect spring afternoon. A light covering of high cloud blocks the presence of direct sunlight, but allows a diffused luminosity to overspread this corner of the island. A gentle breeze falls from the long slopes of the high country behind us, fluttering the outstretched wing feathers of a pair of dancing wandering albatrosses. With their necks sensuously twisting around each other, they wheel and leap in their elegant courtship display. Yet after the joy and romance of the wanderers, comes a dramatic emotional letdown.

In walking along the beach later, instead of staying close to the edge of the sea, I walk at a higher level, treading the hard-packed grey clay where it meets the scrub grass of the dunes. In this region there are many small, saucer-shaped sinkholes, filled with mud, where the underlying surface has dissolved or collapsed. Walking along, my eye is unexpectedly caught by a rippling movement in the depression immediately ahead. As I move closer, the small head of a baby fur seal lifts slowly above the level of the silver-grey sludge. Its eyes hold mine for a second or so as it struggles to free its small body and find some solid footing. There is a moment when the youngster manages to break free with its tail, arc it briefly through the air – but the effort proves too much. It is too exhausted; it sinks lower in the morass, is lost to view, the surface of the mud closing over its sleek body until there is scarcely a ripple to be seen. The fledgeling seal has kept its head above the mire as long as possible – although eyes were closed at the last – until it could no longer support its weight and gave up the struggle. The drama occupies no more than two minutes, yet is as poignant a scene as I have witnessed in the wild.

The hole is no more than four feet by seven across, and I have no idea how deep it might be. My immediate impulse is to get down in there and try to pull it out – although obtaining any purchase on the smooth, mud-slick body would be a problem. As I stand worrying about the situation, the youngster's head once again slowly rises above the surface, eyes opening briefly in response to the light, and the urge to help becomes acute: I feel it as pain in the abdomen. I must act. I kneel over the hole, toes gripping the ground hard, when I feel a restraining hand on my shoulder.

"*Non, monsieur. C'est la vie naturelle . . . n'assistez pas. Je regrette, mais c'est le règle.*"

One of the naturalists from the scientific station is standing above me. I hardly hear what he is saying. I tell him that with two of us there it should be easy to release the seal from its prison. But he just shakes his head and pulls me to my feet; then spreads his hands wide, a grimace suggesting both resignation and exasperation.

I walk away – angrily, I suppose – the mute look of appeal in the seal pup's eyes at the forefront of my mind. Of course, I am aware of the scientific attitude – that there should be no human intervention in natural processes, however sympathetic the motive; I even understand the reasons behind it. Yet why not help? For aren't we creatures of nature also? Isn't our presence in these previously unreachable places due to the natural resources of mind we have intelligently exploited to build ships and travel? Therefore, a helping hand from one of us is a helping hand from nature herself. As the Ancient Greeks would have it, because man represents the highest-evolved intelligence in the natural world, he is the consciousness of nature, her steward; as such it is his *purpose* to intervene and – as Aristotle said – "realize nature's unrealized ends". I despise myself for walking away. Some pictorial images refuse to go away as life moves on: they remain atop the file of visual memories, surfacing unexpectedly, triggered by the most unlikely stimulus. The face of the baby seal on Cap Digby, Iles de Kerguelen, persists like that for me. Time on Kerguelen passes rapidly, as it does on such desolate islands when one is caught up in the exuberant ballet of life. Yet now, moved by the death I have witnessed and was too morally weak to prevent, I cannot wait to leave.

As we pull away from the narrow anchorage, a squadron of black-backed gulls attack a lone giant petrel on patrol. The numerous peninsulas and large bays sheltering legions of islets slip away on the starboard side, together with dark cliffs sheer to the water up which rockhopper penguins miraculously climb to their nests. The high pinnacled crags and ridges reach threateningly out into the ocean, and I catch a last glimpse of the shimmering peak of 6430-foot Mount Ross and its permanent ice cap set among the peaks of the volcanic interior.

Heard Island – Australian territory – is an island with a reputation. An outer sentinel of Antarctica proper, mostly covered by permanent ice which terminates at the sea in ice cliffs 50 to 100 feet high, it is approximately 150 nautical miles south of Kerguelen, and as different from the more northerly archipelago as chalk is from cheese.

Heard is notoriously a bad-weather place. Here the sea is usually rougher, and the wind stronger, than around any of the other subantarctic islands on the "Far Side". Changes in weather conditions are sudden and often unpredictable. When Sir Douglas Mawson took the *Discovery*'s launch ashore on Heard during his 1930–1 expedition, a gale sprang up so quickly and unexpectedly that he was unable to return to the ship for three days – and even then only at the risk of high seas swamping the launch.

The island is nothing more or less than a mountain rising from the ocean – and an actively volcanic one at that, with a newly formed lava lake in the crater similar to that of Mount Erebus. The summit, known as Big Ben, culminates in the cone called Mawson Peak which rises to a height of 9005 feet. It is probably the combination of height, extensive ice fields, volcanic activity, and severe cold that results in the island generating its own weather systems.

The vista it presents from the sea with the ice-covered, smoke-plumed summit of Big Ben, is as dramatic and beautiful as anything in the Southern Ocean. Its extensive and varied wildlife of penguins (macaroni, rockhopper and gentoo), seals (elephant and leopard), and birds (petrels, cormorants, albatrosses) is superbly set off by the imposing slopes of Big Ben.

The sky is overcast, wind gusting up to 60 mph and whipping the sea into whitecaps, snow and sleet showers hampering visibility. The chances of seeing Big Ben unobscured by cloud seem remote.

By 8 am, we have reached the northwest corner of the island and are standing off Sydney Cove where we had hoped to anchor and go ashore.

Heard Island. "The vista it presents from the sea with the ice-covered, smoke-plumed summit of Big Ben, is as dramatic and beautiful as anything in the Southern Ocean."

But the wind is gusting, even more strongly – dangerously so for helicopters; and certainly nearly impossible for inflatables.

Cruising down the leeward side of the island we follow the coastline south and east, keeping, I would say, no more than a quarter-mile from shore. I count no fewer than five major glaciers descending to the sea, although the heights above them are lost in cloud. There is no vegetation here save for a few ice-free areas where moss and a little tussocky grass manage to grow. Crozet and Kerguelen suddenly seem lush, almost tropical, in comparison.

Halfway down the island's east coast the weather begins to improve – the cloud ceiling rising to about two thousand feet, the air becoming clearer. Forward visibility is rapidly improving; and the sea looks blue rather than black. It is difficult to credit such a local change after only four

137

or five miles from the storminess of the north point. The coastline is a confusion of projecting spits, high rock headlands, ice cliffs, all seemingly connected by narrow stone or grass saddles. Heaven help anyone having to get in there in a small boat, I think, remembering Mawson's account of getting on and off the shore with the *Discovery*'s launch.

Ninety minutes and about fifteen sea miles later we are fully abeam of Big Ben and Mawson Peak, but the summit is lost in a vast cloud of heavy white cumulus that overhangs the length of the island at a height of about 5000 feet. In spite of it, there is a stunning five-mile vista of the Brown and Stephenson glaciers where they join to sweep steeply down to the scree and rock of the shore.

Standing off the island the wind is still gusting between 40 and 50 mph; the sea is dancing in choppy powerful waves. It is almost noon, cloud-ceiling increasing to about 6000 feet, some blue sky about and forward visibility excellent. The wind conditions are marginal for helicopter flying, especially when it must come on to the small landing pad of a vessel rolling in rough seas. But Anatoly the senior Russian pilot agrees to fly, for part of our job is to deliver mail to the Australian Meteorological Station, and off he goes looking like a small gnat in the vast panorama of ocean, mountain and ice. Twenty minutes later he is back. He makes a masterly approach and touchdown, fighting the strong eddies of air beating around our stern, holding off until his wheels are perfectly placed for the final drop to the deck.

And then comes a black-backed gull, making all the right moves to follow him in. The bird bides its time, then flies into the wind directly above the centre of the pad, hovers there at a height of about fifteen feet, and with wings beating out great downdrafts of air, descends vertically under perfect control to touch down alongside the now quiet helicopter. For some seconds the bird stands quite still, merely extending its neck and looking around as if expecting applause – an ovation it entirely deserves – then, taking a last look round, lifts easily from the deck and wheels off towards the foreshore.

Heard is now falling away behind, and with the sky still clearing the island assumes its proper aspect as a solitary mountain thrusting up from a great waste of ocean. It is overwhelmingly white – white ice, white slopes, white cloud cover, and a white-water surround. From a position almost due south, the snow-glazed flanks of Big Ben appear to extend in every direction, leaving but a rim of rock and cliff to define the island's perimeter. But the cone of Mawson's Peak is still not visible: at least one thousand feet of the summit remain wreathed in cloud – an impenetrably thick, umbrella-shaped mass which, in size and contour, replicates Heard's silhouette to create a twin island in the sky. Although the wind is freshening, the mountain's covering of cloud seems immovable, anchored by gravity to the glacier and volcanic cone. The swell is also increasing. We are now just beyond the 50th parallel of latitude and approaching the Antarctic Convergence.

8

THE FAR SIDE

The closer we move to latitude 60° south, the shorter and less steep the swell and the weaker the force it delivers. By the following afternoon we have progressed to 62°. Heard is over 600 miles behind us and we are just about into the ice.

At this stage everything "subantarctic" is forgotten. The air is noticeably colder and by mid-morning a light snow is falling; shortly afterwards the first iceberg appears – a castellated and dramatically weathered structure pierced by blue arched tunnels into which the sea surges before being repulsed to emerge in short, choppy waves. Sheer walls rear 70 feet above the ocean, gleaming in the watery light, and continuing unbroken round the quarter-mile or so of the iceberg's circumference.

With the approach of the big bergs, I have noticed that even the most seasoned Antarctic scientist becomes quiet and expectantly intense, as if newly stirred by unfamiliar sensations and provocative thoughts. One has always to remind oneself that with 150 feet of ice showing above the surface, there is an invisible 600 feet or thereabouts beneath. This iceberg, now, has likely broken away from a much larger tabular berg – one that was possibly grounded for some time in coastal fast ice: hence the serrated, egg-box-like weathering of its top surface, and the clean-cut squareness of the wider end. And here it is, the great white catalyst which can sharpen the senses and awaken sensibilities hitherto unrealized.

What will happen to this magnificent white-and-blue berg alongside which we are drifting? Depending on the strength of currents and of that of the winds, it will, at some point, be free of the Antarctic winter and most likely wander north and east in subantarctic latitudes, diminishing in size as warmer salt water eats away at its underside while sea and wind weather its surface. Tunnels have already been bored into it by the swell. Probably it will break up into several small bergs by next summer, and then they in turn will be gone a short time later. Like all beautiful things its existence is ephemeral. One's mind becomes still in its presence.

With the arrival of this first envoy from the vast white continent comes a sense of freedom, the final break from the arrogance of man-centred civilizations – from politics, greed, and the "gross national product" syndrome. This hostile land ahead demands of anyone a radical change in their perspective on the world – we are approaching a place in which human beings are the least adapted creatures to survive its rigors. The power of Antarctica lies in this very fact; we have no natural aptitude for it – it is one of the very few places left where we are not a dominant species.

Ernest Shackleton on entering iceberg "country":

About 3 a.m. on the morning of January 16 (1908), we entered an area of tabular bergs, varying from eighty to one hundred and fifty feet in height, and all the morning we steamed in beautiful weather with a light northerly wind, through the lanes and streets of a wonderful snowy Venice. Tongue and pen fail in attempting to describe the magic of such a scene. . . . A stillness, weird and uncanny, seemed to have fallen upon everything. . . . Some of these bergs had been weathered into the fantastic shapes more characteristic of the Arctic regions, and from peak and spire flashed out the new caught rays of the morning sun. Beautiful as this scene was, it gave rise to some anxiety in my mind, for I knew that if we were caught in a breeze amidst this maze of floating ice, it would go hard with us. . . . We were now revelling in the indescribable freshness of the Antarctic that seems to permeate one's being, and which must be responsible for that longing to go again which assails each returned explorer from polar regions.

The ocean is filling with the advance guard of the pack ice ahead: these are large floes – what the Russians called strip ice – and by evening the sea around is glistening white in all directions as we push ever harder into an increasing density of pack. We are now at latitude 63° south; 350 nautical miles from the Antarctic coast and not very far from the Antarctic Circle – close enough for us to be experiencing almost twenty-four hours of daylight. At 10 pm we are surrounded – not just by heavy ice – but by squadrons of Antarctic petrels and snow petrels. They fly in no particular formation, soaring, diving, and peeling away independently as things in the water catch their eyes. The snow petrels fly more conventionally, beating their wings regularly for propulsion, whereas the larger Antarctic petrel with a long, slim wing not unlike the albatross, sails glider-like, wings merely flexing to use the currents of air, scissoring the water in the open leads on one wing tip, body at 90° to the surface.

For the first time ever I am able to observe the snow petrel at close quarters. A delicately beautiful all-white bird with a wingspan a little less than two feet, it is practically invisible when seen against a backdrop of ice or snow. Yet backed by the pale blue of a summer Antarctic sky it assumes an otherworldly presence, as if it were a visitant from the outer reaches of space.

An hour before midnight . . . and the birds have gone; the whole scene is suffused with a purple-grey afterglow – a haunting and mythic light which intensifies the sense of isolation as sky, sea, and ice flow away and into each other with no visible horizon. This is the magical theatre of the Antarctic which fills one with delight, yet at the same time heightens one's ever-present sense of vulnerability. One would be an easy victim should the drama be taken over by the elemental furies who decide suddenly to streak across the stage. Undercurrents of anxiety threaten the first glow of elation.

The Greeks understood this paradox, recognizing that when joy and fear go hand in hand one must overcome the fear by assuming the mantle of the hero: first find the courage to accept the challenge offered by the dangerous and the unknown, then act confidently to defy the threat at hand, even though the chances of success may be small. In so doing we satisfy something essentially transcendent within us – acknowledge the presence of the spirit and resolve to keep faith with it. This, as I have said, is a very Greek place.

For a queasy sailor, an icebreaker is agony in the open sea, but is a joy when finally in the ice. The sea's movement is tamed by the weight of the pack, and the ship, now completely in her element, is as steady and strong as the proverbial rock. The crashing, crunching, and slithering sounds of the vessel progressing through and over the ice are music to the ears, providing evidence of things solid rather than fluid. In this environment one could literally walk on water – a reassuring thought for those who find the ever-rolling sea difficult to face with equanimity

At 5 am there is an Antarctic petrel flying a mere five or six feet from my window at exactly the same speed as the ship. It keeps its position for several minutes, looking neither right or left, before banking away on one wing and executing a diving turn to the ice. I am immediately reminded of a similar – though far more profound – experience recounted by the noted South African writer Sir Laurens Van der Post.

Sailing from South Africa to England in 1961, Van der Post was resting one afternoon in his cabin. While not fully asleep, nor yet quite awake, he found himself transported, as if in a dream, to stand on the ice of an alpine glacier. Above him was the figure of Carl Gustav Jung, the pre-eminent Swiss doctor and psychologist – an old friend – who, as Laurens looked up, waved a hand, said, "See you soon" and disappeared over the glacier's rim. The following morning Van der Post awoke to find an albatross flying alongside the cabin window, keeping pace with the ship, holding its position with apparent ease. But unlike my petrel, the head of the albatross was turned to allow the bird to look directly into the cabin and stare at its occupant – an attitude it maintained until, a minute or two later, the cabin steward arrived with the breakfast and a copy of the ship's Daily News bulletin.

On running his eye down the list of news items, Van der Post read of Carl Jung's death the previous afternoon.

We are moving more slowly through $^9/_{10}$ths pack ice. As pack ice density is determined by the amount of visible water, the ship's task in dealing with an ocean that is one part of water to nine of ice requires considerably more power; as a result, thick black smoke pours from the high funnel, sullying the pristine air. We are now at latitude 65° 45′ south; some seventy nautical miles from the Mawson Coast in the general vicinity of Enderby Land.

Light snow falls most of the morning as the vessel proceeds at five or six knots in a heavy concentration of ice. Looking down over the side as the ship's weight sends hairline fractures shimmering through the giant floes – stress points which rapidly widen to deep fractures causing the islands of ice to split from top to bottom – I would say the thickness of the pack is approximately twelve feet. The floes themselves are relatively flat-topped, not having the rounded, humped-up appearance that develops when pressure forces have been working on the pack. Suddenly, to our left on a large floe lies a Ross seal, unmoved by our passage and close enough to

Ross Seal. "… the most elegant, as well as the rarest, of seals."

bear out its reputation as the most elegant, as well as the rarest, of seals. Few people ever see this seal – it lies deep in the solid ice away from the warmer, more accessible parts of the continent.

By noon we are stopped. The nose of the ship is firmly locked in impenetrable ice, which in its turn is firmly attached to the shore of the continent. Sometimes in summer large sections of such ice will break away from the land and float out to sea, leaving a narrow tongue still attached to the coast, but it is far too early in the season for this. We are about ten miles

OPPOSITE: *Encounter between emperor chicks and adult Adélie. "…they are as dissimilar as two related species could be. Night and day. Chalk and cheese."*

from land, stationary and marvellously stable. It may be possible for the icebreaker to proceed further, but to attain the full power required from all six engines would consume far too much of our somewhat limited fuel. It would also take a very long time to make any significant progress. Better not to try any further and use the helicopter to make a landing on the coast.

A five-minute helicopter ride takes us first to Klua Point, where, on a frozen bay surrounded by rock bluffs topped by great domed mounds of hard snow are some 15,000 nesting emperors. Then we move to an area a little south and east of Klua Point. Here the impressive, highly fractured slopes of the Sonsdal Glacier stand away behind me to the west. The Vestfold hills fold their icy humps atop one another and disappear into the distance, down the coast, further south and east. And barely a quarter of a mile away lies a small outcrop of weathered rock heavily populated with nesting Adélies.

Emperors and Adélies are the only penguins which spend time below the Antarctic Circle, yet they are as dissimilar as two related species can be. Night and day. Chalk and cheese. Where the emperor is tall, the Adélie is short; the one can weigh ninety pounds. the other eleven. The behaviour of the larger bird is stately and considered: that of the smaller, frenetic and skittish. Unlike the emperor, the Adélie does not suffer the Antarctic winter, but where it goes is a matter of much speculation – probably hundreds of miles north of the winter ice. It is quite likely the Adélies find floes in the open water of the Southern Ocean and remain there feeding until their return in the spring.

Adélie chicks come to maturity over the brief Antarctic summer. The female will lay one or two eggs, the male sharing the incubation and parental duties once the chicks are hatched. His main responsibility, however, is to build and maintain the small scruffy nest of highly prized and fought-over stones.

In a land where there is only rock, ice, snow and water, a perfectly shaped, ideally sized stone is the most precious commodity there is. Unsurprisingly, thievery is rampant throughout the colony. Many years ago scientists placed painted stones at one end of an Adélie rookery and found that, within a week, the stones had made it all the way to the other end. Recent evidence has come to light that female Adélies, long considered monogamous, may engage in a form of prostitution, exchanging casual sexual favours with any male who can offer them a decent rock!

There is only one male in my immediate area, standing alongside his

Adélies jumping. "Most of the others are returning from fishing, jumping acrobatically over the rocks on the way to their nests."

nest of small stones and in constant attendance on his mate. Most of the others are returning from fishing, jumping acrobatically over the rocks on the way to their nests. Frequently and regularly the solitary male leans over to touch her with his beak before circling the nest, surveying its construction like a master builder. Any pebble out of line is potentially vulnerable to a thieving neighbour, stones which have moved or rolled away must be promptly retrieved and repositioned. Meanwhile, she – sitting on her egg – receives this attention with apparent indifference.

After each circuit, the little male waddles a few feet from the nest and digging in a cleft between rock ledges unearths stones of various sizes. Few are abandoned – only those which are awkwardly shaped or clearly too large. Then he returns with the offering and walks slowly around the nest until at last he deliberately places it into the perfect spot. His mate observes and, one hopes, approves.

Like all inhabitants of the rookery, he too decides from time to time that it is easier simply to fetch a stone from a nearby nest. He tries it now, but immediately becomes the hapless recipient of his neighbour's wild and justifiable wrath. Unfazed, he shakes himself briskly and goes off to dig elsewhere.

Now he returns, carrying the largest rock, looking filthy from the effort of prising it from the frozen ground. This is not a casual rock. This is a rock to be treasured and treated with exceptional care. Round and round he goes, his mate watching his every step. Finally, after an agony of deliberation he finds the place to put it; he finds, too, that the stone is stuck in his beak.

He lowers his head to the ground, but is unable to open his mouth that extra fraction of an inch which would allow gravity to assist. For several minutes he tries everything possible to dislodge the stone, dropping his head, shaking it, banging the stone, twisting his bill. Then, with an absolutely immense effort, where one could almost hear the cracking of his jaws, he manages to open his mouth that extra little bit and the stone falls to the ground.

Slowly, end over end, it starts to roll down the hill away from him. Unbelievingly, he watches it tumble, picking up speed until it comes to rest in a gully perhaps fifteen feet away. Once again, he must descend the hill and retrieve it from the narrow slot into which it has fallen; but this time he takes it by the corner only, then delicately and firmly puts it in its spot. The female turns to acknowledge his effort. He straightens up, touches her back with his bill and, after this brief moment of intimacy, starts off again on his ceaseless rounds.

Busy little creatures. Life on the run all around Antarctica. And a remarkably successful life, to judge by the thousands of birds cramming the rookeries of the continent. These tough little penguins have succeeded in nature's most wicked climate and, so far, in spite of the increased presence and often heavy hand of man. To date, they have withstood tourists, airstrips, attempts at commercial harvesting, being used as food at certain bases, oil spills, garbage and competition from krill factory ships for their food supply.

I ask a friend who works with the Australian National Antarctic Research Expeditions in this region how long it would take me to proceed ten miles down the coast under the present summer conditions. His reply is

OPPOSITE: *Adélie with rock. "This is not a casual rock. This is a rock to be treasured and treated with exceptional care."*

that first I would find it impossible to maintain a heading. Having to negotiate an obstacle course of fast ice and grounded icebergs means I would be going up and down, zigzagging in every direction. Within an hour I would become totally disoriented, not to mention tired out. Then I might fall through a crack in the ice and freeze in a matter of minutes; tumble and injure myself while clambering around the ends of grounded icebergs; find the ice cap unattainable because of the fissures, many up to 100-feet deep, which form where its edge meets the fast ice of the sea. Finally, if I did make it to the surface of the mainland, there were unstable snow bridges over crevasses and the icy tongues of glaciers to traverse. Progress on such terrain is excruciatingly slow – many hours to the mile – three days for ten miles if I was extremely fit, well-equipped and lucky.

I look on the Adélie with a great deal of respect. This, after all, is the land he calls home.

As our helicopter continues south and east, the clarity of air and range of visibility is spellbinding – a crystal whiteness moving away into an infinity of pastel blue sky. Flying at about 1000 feet in this crystalline air, it is possible to see for eighty or more miles in any direction. The relatively open water through which we have sailed in the early morning – before the pack closed in – is just visible to the north, perhaps three hours sailing time away; while the coastline of Enderby Land stretches away to east and west and into infinity.

Now I see the curvature and full scale of the ice cap for the first time as it rises from fractured cliffs at the edge of the frozen sea to the limits of my southward vision: a glistening mantle of ice stretching away from the sea without interruption in every direction. From above, it is possible to discern how the relative shallowness of the ice at the rookery permits it to be shaped by the bedrock beneath, and allows the rock to break through as intrusive *nunataks* – peaks of hills surrounded by permanent ice.

From a height of 500 feet, this spectacular, dome-like field of ice rolling away as far as the eye can see towards the South Pole, is the classic image one has of Antarctica. All along this "Far Side" coast the landscape hardly varies. Only in the western environs of the Amery Ice Shelf, in the area of Prydz Bay, do notable outcrops of rock and mountains – which, more realistically should be called hills – become part of the scene; yet they are never more than minor blots on this vast spread of glittering ice.

That the geography of the eastern seaboard continues in similar vein, for hundreds of miles, is borne out by accounts of Sir Douglas Mawson's 1931 expedition which fought its way up this same coast from the opposite direction, steaming west from Cape Adare. The pack ice was heavy and widespread that year, and only from time to time was his ship, the *Discovery*, able to get near enough to the continent to see the land, never mind put men ashore. But Mawson had the advantage of carrying a small aeroplane aboard – a Moth biplane fitted with floats – which allowed him to make observations, weather permitting, of coastal regions far to the east and south. Both Mawson and Group Captain Douglas – one of the two pilots – describe the land as seen from 6000 feet as a dome of ice rising to a plateau of 4000 feet, frequently broken by bare rock.

Thus the overall appearance of long stretches of maritime East Antarctica, stands in stark contrast to the precipitous Alpine grandeur of the Peninsula and West Coast.

Any comparison of Antarctica's two sides must involve some mention of sea ice. Much depends on the nature of each year's summer weather – warming temperatures or otherwise; calm or stormy seas – pertaining to each region. On his 1929–30 expedition from Cape Town to East Antarctica, Mawson, for example, ran into gale conditions almost daily, where we have daily had blue skies, mild temperatures and gentle winds. He was stopped frequently by impenetrable $^{10}/_{10}$ ths pack ice. We have been able to proceed through relatively open water.

But once through the pack and nearing the coast, there is still the fast ice to contend with. And that is a different story. Often it thrusts twenty-five or thirty miles out from the land for many hundreds of miles – a far-ranging barrier of ice, anchored to the land and often to parts of the ocean floor, which consistently hugs long stretches of East Antarctica's coastline, never completely disappearing even in the mildest years. On the other hand, there are many summers in West Antarctica when the coastal waters are almost completely free of pack ice, and fast ice is reduced to relatively narrow shoreline strips.

At a distance of about half-a-mile from our position off MacRobertson land, a large tabular iceberg lies grounded. Its sheer walls rise from the surface of the fast ice to a height of about 100 feet and, with a likely four fifths of its height submerged, this would suggest an ocean depth of some 400 feet at the point of grounding. Many hairline cracks – vertical and

horizontal – travel over its surface, a bright frozen facade, bearing like an ageing beauty the ravages of sun, wind and water. A huge circular cavity spirals its way toward the heart of the berg – a high round-arched entrance rivalling, were it set in stone, the grandest doorways found in Romanesque churches. What is even more striking is the purity and intensity of colour which bleeds away from the entrance to the depths of the iceberg's interior – a scale of translucent blues ranging from the palest of cerulean at the outer face, to the richest cobalt within the deepest recesses.

Conditions seem to be perfect for a walk on the ice, but once again the clarity of air and light plays tricks with one's sense of distance. After we have walked for ten minutes the grounded berg seems to be just as far away; another ten, and still a very long way to go. It must be getting on for over a mile away. Three figures have already reached the iceberg's base and are standing beneath the blue cave – "the blue grotto", as I call it. With their presence providing a scale, it can be seen that the cave is simply enormous and, suddenly, rather frightening: the men look ant-like in comparison. They are trying to climb the series of short ice cliffs which give access first to the entrance and then to the deep blue tunnel. The short ascents are proving difficult. Two men fall repeatedly and give up; the third slithers his way over the lip of the final stage and disappears inside.

At this point I double my estimate of the berg's height. I am about to move forward when a large crack opens up in the ice ahead – quite silently – then runs for about 100 feet before petering out. I hear odd hissings and faint cracklings from deep beneath our feet. There is more movement of the ice. The crack that has run from just ahead of my position begins to widen; then it settles down and temporarily stabilizes when some nine inches wide and a foot deep. I imagine I can hear the ebb and flow of the tides far below where I am standing.

Taking care to stride as widely as possible across the newly created tide-crack, I suddenly descend knee-deep into damp and slushy ice on the other side. Slowly I extricate myself, one foot at a time, find firm ice and retreat more carefully. The two men who tried to scale the ice cliffs into the blue

OPPOSITE: *The Blue Grotto. "A huge circular cavity spirals its way toward the heart of the berg – a high round-arched entrance rivalling, were it set in stone, the grandest doorways found in Romanesque churches."*

grotto are on their way back, tiny figures still. There is no sign of the third member of the party.

For the first time I take serious notice of the large fissures running diagonally up and away from the under-rim of the cave's high arch – ominous signs that the weight of ice above is bearing down and weakening the opening. How much longer can the span support such a mass?

Hairline tide cracks are now much more in evidence; as yet they show no signs of opening, but it is just a matter of time. Possibly within a few weeks the fast ice on which I am walking will break clear and drift off to join the pack lingering out at sea.

And the man in the blue grotto? He is a glaciologist who, on his return some time later, tells of a deeply crevassed and serrated tunnel floor, difficult and dangerous to traverse and running directly into the interior of the iceberg – an interior so darkly blue that staring into it effectively blinded him to all points of spatial reference. It was like diving into a dark ocean cave: he lost all sense of position – up or down, left or right – so much so that he had to talk himself out of there, tell himself that the light blue ice lay to his rear and represented "out"; the dark blue ice was at his front and meant "in". The deathly cold inhibited reason and clouded judgement: another five minutes, he said, would have had him sitting down, back against the wall, incapable of movement like an autistic child.

Several Adélies escort me on the walk back, maintaining a parallel course about ten paces away to my left. When I stop, they stop; watch me curiously, flippers outstretched, heads on one side. After all, when, if ever, had they seen oversized bipeds wandering around on fast ice in these remote parts?

The evening sky diffuses a glow like old ivory lightly brushed with gold. In my mind this landscape has become a mythic sea where every gleaming iceberg is a deserted and castellated island. It is a setting for an archaic drama, but without a human character on stage. The purity of light and windswept snow removes all thoughts of man. It is a beauty and purity which gives both pleasure and anxiety: pleasure in the beauty, unease in the purity – for the pure is the sterile and sterility is death. Where to die? Warm room, white sheets? Or cold ice cave beneath a mantle of frost?

Adélies stand around – sculpted pieces on an ivory-white chessboard which climbs into the sky.

9

THE MONOLITHS AND
THE EMPERORS OF EAST
ANTARCTICA

A pale sapphire-blue sky looks down on a sea the colour of blue-black ink. Brilliant snow-covered ice, streaked by jet-black threads of near freezing water, stretches to the horizon. We are escorted by Antarctic and snow petrels soaring and side-slipping between sea and sky.

By mid-morning tabular icebergs of all shapes and sizes encircle us; as the day progresses the ice glare becomes unendurable without the protection of dark glasses The sensation is one of drifting and dreaming as if lost in a Fellini film where the soundtrack is muted, camera lens not quite focused. Time passes in and out of consciousness. There is nothing in our world but sun and ice and water.

As evening falls a wedge of sky immediately above the horizon takes on the texture of satin and shines like burnished bronze; overhead, wisps of white cloud – high altitude ice crystals – streak across the firmament from east to west, and the pack ice is growing denser. Low moans surge from the northeast, driving flecks of surface snow to scurry through the air like spindrift flung from the wave crests of rough sea.

By 3 am the light is already growing to full daytime brilliance. The distance south and east from the Blue Grotto position to our next landfall – the Scullin Monolith – is about 140 nautical miles. Although the weather is still benign, this is the region where Sir Douglas Mawson's 1929–30 expedition was beset – and at this same time of year – by gale-force winds and near blizzard conditions. It was also in this area where the chartered Swedish ship *Kista Dan* which had carried the men and equipment to establish Mawson Base in 1954 was, on its return in late summer, caught in enormous seas – described by Dr André Migot, a French physician aboard, as follows: ". . . enormous waves, entirely covered with a skin of ice, smashing on the deck and showering the ship with splinters of ice. The

Kista Dan struggled gallantly against the storm, and Captain Peterson made desperate efforts to keep her head on to the waves, but by midnight the wind had reached a speed of ninety miles an hour or more, and it became quite impossible to control the ship. We had unloaded all our cargo at Mawson, and the ship was now riding high out of the water, and offering such a large area to the wind that it was no longer possible to resist its growing force. The limit had been passed: the ship no longer obeyed the helm and had begun to drift sideways through a sea bristling with icebergs – a mere toy at the mercy of the storm." Somehow they survived, although there were, and still are, no charts for this area.

By noon the coastline of the continent is in full view. The fierce bastion of the Scullin Monolith and its flanking nunataks, hovering like acolytes, rise defiantly from the icy flatness. This impressive tower of folded and streaked metamorphic rock, glistening with garnets, stands like the keep of a lost castle guarding both land and sea. It is the last relatively freestanding buttress in a short string of vertical outcrops; its northern wall descends into the ocean, the southern to the continental ice cap. Rising to a height of 1347 feet it stands as a marvellous vertical anomaly on an otherwise horizontal and featureless seascape.

The visibility is perfect. For the first time since reaching the coastal regions of East Antarctica I find it is possible to distinguish clearly the edge of the mainland ice cap where it falls, vertical and sheer, to the fast ice below. At first, I estimate the height of these frozen cliffs in the immediate vicinity to reach sixty or seventy feet. Then on flying over them, their true scale becomes apparent. Once again, I am hopelessly wrong – they are at least twice as high as my original estimate. They are heavily indented on the vertical face by concertina-like ravines cutting deeply into the ice, and the top surfaces are scored by crevasses or canyons – I cannot tell the difference – dropping steeply into the depths. It is impossible to imagine how one could ever cross such fissures, either ascending from the fast ice or descending from the ice cap. The continent's edge is so forbidding at this point that I desperately will the helicopter to get the hell out of it – to rise well above such dangerous terrain and head inland.

At that moment the machine goes straight up, making no attempt to move forward over the ice field. The razored details of the barrier beneath us grow less distinct. To my surprise the pilot is taking us straight up the side of the monolith as if he were flying an elevator. The ascent is long

156

The Scullin Monolith from thirty miles out in the pack ice. "This impressive tower of folded and streaked metamorphic rock, glistening with garnets, stands like the keep of a lost castle guarding both land and sea."

and nerve-wracking: there seems to be no summit to the massive wall of rock just outside the window.

I am concerned with the unpredictability of the winds. Large, open expanses of ice spreading to interior uplands can generate their own weather, particularly in the form of sudden windstorms – katabatic or gravity winds, caused by cold compact air rolling downward from high glaciers or plateaus of ice and gusting at high speed. A helicopter trying to land or lift off from a 1400-foot peak would be dashed out of the sky. Even if caught just sitting up there the machine would likely be blown away. Once we are up, we are very much up with, realistically, no prospect of successfully climbing down, nor negotiating the ice cliffs.

So, we land on top of the monolith – this geological feature named by

Metamorphic rock, Scullin Monolith. "A summit made up of gnarled and knotted rock."

Mawson after James H. Scullin, Prime Minister of Australia from 1929 to 1931. Mawson had sighted the peak and its adjacent rock ridge on a reconnaissance flight over the coast of MacRobertson Land on 5 January 1930, during the course of his first exploratory voyage to East Antarctica.

The total area atop the monolith is surprisingly spacious – about the size of one and a half tennis courts – and the helicopter has found the only level and boulder-free patch available on a summit made up of gnarled and knotted rock. To the north our perch rises like a rampart to face the frozen sea; if one moves south – a short boulder-hopping climb – the surface drops away in the form of a low-lying saddle which connects steeply with the next highest point in the small range of peaks. But to the east the rock falls away, with no protective crest to provide a sense of spatial security. The rock slopes down and out – pulling the eye the full length of an 80° slope of scree and slab to the faraway surface of the ice cap, and the horrific fall of its cliffs to the sea. On the west the drop is mercifully hidden by the rise of the ground and the natural piling of ridge and loose stones, but the glassy rolling fields of the ice sheet are visible for miles along the westering coast. I start to reconnoitre the perimeter;

mainly to convince myself that I am actually on top of this bloody great plinth sticking out of the ice in the middle of nowhere.

Then come the birds: first the skuas which take no finding at all, and begin to act rather threateningly; then the Antarctic and snow petrels which have to be searched out. Crossing from Scullin via the saddle and moving upward to the adjacent peak is a difficult climb. It is not that the slope is dangerously steep or exceptionally long, but it is a mad jumble of large boulders. What little space exists between them is filled with patches of snow and soft grey-green lichen growing in the more protected cracks. Once at the summit one enters a vast colony of Antarctic petrels, their thousands of nests so closely spaced that it is necessary to be extremely careful not to step on an incubating bird.

The nesting adults take small notice of anyone, remaining motionless while their partners, who circle overhead, raise a din of repeated calling: a sound which comes and goes like a wordless chorale. These birds with their long, distinctively marked black-and-white wings and short, stubby tails, spend all their lives at sea save for the breeding season. Able to cope in the severest storms the Southern Ocean can produce, they navigate beautifully over the rising and falling waters using the wind and air pressures created along wave fronts, gliding, banking, endlessly scissoring the surface of the sea on first one wing tip then the other.

At the next ridge the ground falls away steeply – a sheer drop all the way to the land ice. Nesting in small pockets in the rock, and on the narrowest of ledges, is a colony of southern fulmars – the wild white birds of Peter I. Mixed in with them are many of the small, elegant snow petrels who have managed to find small nesting holes in the rock where none would seem to exist. The view down the cliff face is a black and white kaleidoscope of ruffling feathers and gently bobbing heads. All this warm-blooded avian life is a reminder that while the land may be barren, the sea is not; that these thousands of birds, petrels and fulmars – visiting for the breeding season – draw their sustenance from the cold waters of the Southern Ocean – waters rich in krill, squid and fish.

The afternoon passes quickly; it is 5 pm before I return – visibly sagging at the knees – to the improvised helicopter pad: the climb down from boulder to boulder has proved to be far more wearisome than the earlier ascent. A sudden gust of wind blows my hair. There is a lull. Then another quick blow. It comes from the west, across sea and ice, cold on the cheek, and a bar of

Southern fulmar. "The view down the cliff face is a black and white kaleidoscope of ruffling feathers and gently bobbing heads."

dark cloud suddenly appears on the far horizon. My concern is that these gusts may herald the arrival of katabatic winds – windstorms common enough in this sort of high-stretching icy environment, and dangerous for helicopters flying, as I've previously noted. A skua stands high on the rock behind me. Wings fully extended, head held high and carnivorous beak in full scimitar-like profile, in this light it is an imperial, even heraldic, creature.

There is no helicopter waiting. Brief moment of panic. The pilot must have seen the weather coming and, knowing the vulnerability of a helicopter in strong winds, has beaten a hasty retreat.

"He's buggered off," I say to myself somewhat wildly. Yet when I look to the west a few minutes later the sky is clear and bright – not a sign of the storm bar which had threatened just a few moments before. Five minutes later and the helicopter comes whirring back in the fading light. The imperial skuas take rapidly to the air, and I with equal alacrity to the 'copter.

Adélies coming ashore at the foot of the Murray Monolith. "... Adélies come porpoising to hurl themselves, with wild abandon, out of the water and on to the ice."

Lifting off, the pilot swings high over Scullin, now rapidly becoming a mere pinpoint of rock in the vast desert of ice.

Later in the evening open water appears giving direct access to the Murray monolith – a somewhat lesser formation a few miles down the coast to the east. A large Adélie rookery has established itself on the snow and ice which cling to the base of Murray's lower slopes. Alongside the monolith a glacier pushes a tongue dramatically out to sea, forming a small bay into which hundreds of Adélies come porpoising to hurl themselves, with wild abandon, out of the water and on to the ice. The Adélie is able to lift itself six feet or more above the surface of the water, but the surface itself does not seem to afford them much of a purchase. They explode from well beneath it, arching their bodies backwards with their tails extended, feet and flippers tucked in, and their heads and beaks slightly raised in a

161

purposive thrust. Only as they prepare for touchdown do they look at the ground, push their feet forward, and extend their flippers for balance. Most landings are not elegant; sometimes they fall back into the sea and have to try again, or slide down the ice, their feet slipping out from underneath them. On landing – elegantly done or not – they simply pick themselves up and make a beeline for home.

Adélies coming from the sea at Murray have to struggle up a 45° ice slope to reach the bare rock nesting site above the snow line. Shoulders hunched, and using a sideways swaying motion to give increased thrust, they work very hard to get where they're going. As nesting pairs change duties – either to sit on the egg or to go off to fish – a continuous line of busy, dogged penguins trudge up the slope while another line, equally doggedly, sways their way down.

By midnight the light and colour of the scene is magical. Clouds pass overhead, suffused with a golden-pink hue – a glow which is picked up by the pure white surface of the glacier's higher reaches. In contrast, the lower flanks reflect the deep sovereign blue of the evening sea; it is a stunningly beautiful juxtaposition of colour and light.

Yet I am told that only a few days ago the entire region was utterly inaccessible, icebound and beset by blizzards and dangerous gales.

The plan is to proceed ever more easterly down the coast of Mawson Land – a region well known for its massed icebergs and heavy pack – in order to approach and round Cape Darnley. Once the cape is doubled, we will head almost due south into Mackenzie Bay with MacRobertson Land to the right, and the northwest point of the Amery Ice Shelf straight ahead at a distance of about 100 nautical miles. If this can be accomplished despite the heavy pack, we should be able to proceed for about 130 miles east and south along the face of Amery, the fastest moving shelf of ice in the world. Should this course prove impossible, then we will continue to ply eastward beyond Cape Darnley before, hopefully, turning south again to intersect the ice shelf further along.

The Amery Ice Shelf is perhaps only one-seventh the size of the Ross Ice Shelf in West Antarctica – yet at approximately 130 miles broad at its sea-facing end, and 250 miles long measuring from the limits of the glacier which feeds it, the shelf is still an impressive mass of floating ice which fills a major part of Mackenzie Bay.

Statistics by themselves cannot convey the full effect of a natural phenomenon, although they may certainly aid one's appreciation of it. The Amery Ice Shelf is fed by the Lambert Glacier which has been described as the largest valley glacier, or ice stream, in the world. It is possible to follow its surface flow lines 250 miles upglacier: soundings in the middle of the glacier reveal a depth of over 8000 feet of ice, and the centre line velocity – ice flow per year – is 1127 feet. These are formidable numbers. When this flow becomes part of the Amery Ice Shelf, the shelf's own centre line velocity is measured at 3900 feet of flow per year – representing a yearly movement of almost three-quarters of a mile. Hence the description of Amery as the fastest moving ice shelf in the world.

The Lambert Glacier-Amery Ice Shelf drainage system is a tremendous complex, one of the largest on the whole Antarctic ice sheet. Writing in their book *Glaciers*, Michael Hambrey and Jürg Alean state that, "A major surge by the Lambert Glacier . . . into the Southern Ocean would have a drastic effect on the world's weather, and as the ice broke up, huge volumes of water would be released, raising the sea level globally by several metres."

But the chances of seeing "the Amery" seem to be getting more and more remote. The pack is closing: open water leads are narrowing and becoming fewer in number. The thickness of the ice around us is between eight and ten feet.

All afternoon the push through the pack continues. It is a numbing stream of sight and sound – broken floes, wildly careening against each other with sharp cracks and deep roars. The sea, released, hisses like a kettle on the boil and swirls up in small whirlpools against the side of each upthrust. Layers of green ice, hitherto submerged, catch the sun to flash iridescent emerald blinks illuminating the black depths of the ocean.

With the passing of every hour it becomes obvious that the pack is becoming denser with still fewer leads of open water to be seen. By early evening our progress has slowed to less than walking pace. We are now deep into $^{10}/_{10}$ ths pack ice. Further progress demands that the ship reverse into the open water previously cleared, then run forward into the ice at speed, riding on to the surface and crushing it from above until stopped by the thickness of the pack.

By early evening it is obvious that we will not reach even the Amery's northwest corner. Over the years, it has been generally agreed by both whaling captains and expedition masters that to meet such heavy pack at this distance from the mainland indicates the presence of extensive, and probably impenetrable, ice ahead. If this should be the case we can spare neither the time nor the fuel in attempting to break through it, even if it were possible for the icebreaker to do so.

At about 7 pm it is obvious that we have completely stopped: one last reverse, one more forward thrust, and the ship has come to a shuddering halt. The abruptly arrested movement, and the sudden silence, are startling. Any stoppage at sea is alarming, but being locked into the ice in this location is especially so. I remind myself that it is early in the season, with two full months of summer to go. The combination of warmer air and a gale or two will likely have the pack broken up and on its way before too long. Yet it takes a few seconds for one's ears to pick up the residual cracking of still breaking ice – like lingering radio static – and distinguish the reassuring hum of the ship's engines: the engine room is still going strong.

Some distance away over the frozen sea, a long line of emperor penguins is tobogganing toward us – a welcoming committee of sorts, as a wag of a New Zealand volcanologist suggests – the local search and rescue squad.

Their arrival, out of the blue as it were, reminds me of a strange passage concerning emperors in André Migot's *Thin Edge of the World*. He describes an incident when the *Kista Dan* – during its journey back to Australia – was virtually stationary in newly forming, very early winter ice. There was no immediate danger and the crew knew it would be possible to push a way through to open water not very far away. They were just "resting up", as it were. That evening an "aurora australis" or "southern lights" was reported and all rushed on deck. This is how Dr Migot described the scene:

> The whole icy landscape was brilliantly lit, and when I turned my head I saw another sight which I found comic but at the same time rather touching: on a great floe which lay almost alongside the ship there were a dozen emperor penguins standing quite still. They seemed to be watching the aurora australis as solemnly as we were. Or had they been attracted by our concert? Possibly, for it is known that they are very fond of music. To prove it to us Dr. Law fetched his accordion and began to play "The Dead Leaves," one of his favourite songs. There was no doubt that the penguins were interested: they stretched out their necks and turned their heads on one side as if trying to hear better. Little by little they waddled nearer the ship's

Fast ice and grounded icebergs where icebreaker was trapped. "Some distance away over the frozen sea, a long line of emperor penguins is tobogganing toward us ..."

side, and then other penguins turned up which we had not seen before, and soon there were about twenty of them, an ecstatic little group only a few yards away. But it was bitterly cold, so in spite of the splendid aurora which still blazed with all its lights, we had to leave off serenading the penguins and go down to our cabins.

By now we have a second group of visitors – a party of very curious Adélies who wander around inspecting the ship as well as scrutinizing some crew who have descended to the ice. I have never seen Adélie penguins in the more accessible regions – the Peninsula, for example – behaving in such a bold and inquisitive fashion. Is it possible that penguins which breed in remote and impenetrable regions are more conditioned by their isolation to pay particular attention to the unusual? These Adélies which have appeared around our stationary ship seem to have come from nowhere to find us – and have certainly wasted little time in checking us out.

Within five minutes the sky's pearl-grey light has lost its clear sheen and the air temperature has dropped. Wedges of dark cloud, purple tinged, lift from the horizon to hang sombrely over the backdrop of grounded bergs – some tilted and tabular, others domed like frozen mosques – the whole being so disposed as to suggest the walls of a vast amphitheatre with us at the centre. For a few moments the lowering cloud holds a hint of menace – as if the stage is being set for the sudden onset of a storm. But then the rays of the late night sun break from the cloud to spill a cascade of bronze-gold light on to the ice walls surrounding us. The illumination diffuses rapidly – as will a wash of colour when spread with a large brush over damp paper, part magenta, part umber – flooding the world in a strange other-worldly glow.

I drift about on the sea ice in soundless slow motion, and were it not for the chill of cold air seeking out the bones of the face, one's body is easily forgotten: time slips away, gravity loses its hold under the combined influences of colour, light and space.

Meanwhile, the abrupt chill has frozen the ice more tightly around the ship. Astern, the spill of broken ice created on our entry into the heavier pack is now ridged and solid. It takes two and a half hours to turn the icebreaker and escape through the narrow, newly frozen land behind us. By midnight, beneath a slate-grey sky, we are moving east and very slightly north through a sea scattered with loose pack and flotillas of flat-topped bergs. In the waning light two emperor penguins suddenly appear as if to salute our departure and bid farewell.

The next morning finds the pack becoming increasingly resistant. A light mist fogs the lower air allowing about 200 yards of forward visibility – the sun just faintly discernible shining above the haze.

As the sun warms, the sea fret slowly begins to disperse. We are completely surrounded by pack ice as far as one can see – snow-covered ice averaging eight feet in depth. We proceed slowly at about six knots. Once again I am amused at the behaviour of the Adélies out on the ice – their panic on catching sight of us causes them to skitter madly over the floe in the direction of the nearest open water, flippers flapping deliriously; then, as if to a silent command, some stop and turn, stare intently at us before flinging themselves into the water like arrows spilled from a quiver.

I wonder why it is that the Adélie population changes so dramatically from floe to floe – whether there are any social dynamics at work that would have one solitary bird occupying a large area of floating ice, no more than two or three standing around on a smaller piece, while as many as a dozen or more would be found clustered on a relatively tiny floe. One might assume that such groupings must surely be the result of random movements, yet this pattern repeats constantly as we work our way through the ice. On

166

one occasion a lone Adélie, standing in the middle of a floe, moves slowly across the ice to the water on the other side. It walks in a hangdog kind of way, casting one or two backward looks at an adjacent floe supporting half-a-dozen birds who are moving with considerably more speed. Head down, back slightly hunched, the solitary penguin appears spiritless, fed up with things, as if it were an outcast from the community of birds.

A few minutes later we pass the first leopard seal I have ever seen out of the water, stretched out on a small floe forty or fifty feet off to the left. The animal, unlike the penguins, makes no attempt to take to the sea – in fact it stares us down as we pass, its needle-like teeth very much in evidence.

By mid-afternoon the pack ice has become more of an obstacle – $^8/_{10}$ths to $^9/_{10}$ths density. The sky is grey, with hints of a lurking sun above thin high cloud; and the air is now extremely cold.

An Antarctic petrel glides alongside, floating over the rail of the main deck. I am startled to see a faint film of ice covering the top surface of its wings and I wait for it to come around again in order to confirm that it is indeed showing signs of icing up. But it does not return, and I am left wondering how frequently this phenomenon occurs: whether the ice could continue to build up, and how the petrel would stay in the air and manoeuvre under such conditions. Icing up – ice forming on the mainplane and control surfaces– renders an aeroplane as manageable as a stone.

The ship is making just sufficient headway to have the ice cracking and popping in every direction, and the plaintive whine of wind rustles over the high superstructure. The density of the pack does not moderate until after midnight. I am fascinated by patterns of fracture lines advancing over each giant floe as the icebreaker's weight bears down. I realize that if I were to go over the rail I could keep up with the ship by walking at a normal pace. After almost twenty-four hours of being caught in this icy prison, it seems natural enough to consider walking with the vessel for a change. So with leads becoming less and less in evidence, it comes as a surprise when a smaller floe succumbs more quickly than usual, and water wells into view – a reminder that one is, in fact, on a ship and not riding a tracked, ice-crawling land vehicle.

At 2 am next day – in light that is more suited to midday than to midnight – we finally emerge from the pack into the open waters of Prydtz Bay. Unhappily, we have also left the Amery Ice Shelf behind us. The extent of fast ice stretching from the coast has prevented us approaching to within even viewing distance of this giant ice system. The very idea of turning Cape Darnley to get in close now seems to have been just so much wishful thinking.

On the second B.A.N.Z.A.R.E. voyage on 3 January 1931, Mawson was not far from our own position when he turned away from the Amery Ice Shelf in foul weather. He wrote:

Since my last message Providence has sustained our best efforts to cope with an exceptional hurricane which struck the Discovery under most inopportune circumstances. The blizzard we thought to weather out in the pack . . . developed into a full hurricane from the south east. We were then almost at the southern edge of the pack facing open berg-strewn waters . . . which waters were lashed into fury, consolidating the pack into a grinding mass against the ship. This pack was of no ordinary nature, but composed largely weather-worn masses the size of Atlantic bergs. Our position being thus untenable, the Discovery escaped from the pack into the freezing waters seething under the lash of wind. The wind increased rapidly to 70 m.p.h. . . . Frozen spindrift and fleecing snow obscured the view so effectually that only by a miracle had we missed crashing into a gigantic tabular berg which loomed up about a length ahead. With the bergs and pack behind us we could not run from the wind. . . .

During this last week of weather the Apollo of these far southern latitudes has run many wonderful atmospheric changes in his march across the sky: effects of light and cloud that cry out for gorgeous music to accompany them – soaring melodies of Beethoven, Wagner, Sibelius . . . or, at times, the ethereal harmonies of Bach and Mozart. Now, once again, we are met by an exquisite sky, separated from the horizon by a broad band of blanched, limpid pink – the colour being reflected by the fast ice near the coast, imparting the ambiance of a seaside, holiday resort to Zhong Shan, the small Chinese scientific base.

Zhong Shan stays in my mind for two reasons, neither of which has anything to do with the base itself. First, there are the skuas, quickly on the scene, as always, and more than usually bold. Secondly, there are the icebergs.

Our helicopter rises to 600 feet, flying across sea ice that is criss-crossed with pressure ridges, the force of which has piled ice blocks one atop the

Grounded icebergs, Chinese base. "The massed bergs appear to have ploughed into the land and become part of it – a pile of crenellated battlements, gabled roofs, high chimneys, and steeply-angled walls."

other to form high extended spines crawling across the frozen sea. We climb another 300 feet to surmount an Alpine range of ice – not just one or two icebergs, but dozens, spreading west and east, and all grounded as if brought in on some huge tidal wave that has jammed them crazily together – old ice that has suffered extremes of weathering, worn down to form pinnacles, buttressing outcrops with gargoyle-like accretions, sweeping slopes, holes and caves. One berg in particular rises at least 200 feet, tilted heavily to the right with a top surface area about the size of two football fields. It bristles with parallel rows of knobs not unlike huge blunted teeth – projections fifty feet tall which, seen from above, give the iceberg's crown the appearance of a giant open egg-box. The deep grid of gullies separating these projections shows blue in their depths, while the square tops of the protrusions themselves gleam white with new snow. It is an iridescent, high-relief chessboard on such a scale – so startlingly surreal – that it seems the plaything of giants.

On landing by the huts that comprise the base I stand stock still. The mind momentarily draws a blank. Straight ahead the continent spreads in broad, gleaming uplands formed of folded ice sheets, relieved in the middle distance by outcrops of bare, honey-coloured rock; to the right a shining and misted glacier tumbles from the heights. To the east, a large medieval city of ice reflects the luminosity of a cold but benevolent sun.

The massed bergs appear to have ploughed into the land and become part of it – a pile of crenellated battlements, gabled roofs, high chimneys, and steeply-angled walls. I am tempted to start walking ahead, out over the ice to stand at the centre of this great open space ringed by glacier and a "cityscape" of icebergs – and then turn slowly through the circle and let every detail of form and colour register its unique appeal. Yet remembering my rash wanderings around Mount Erebus at Cape Evans, and how easily one's senses are consistently misled by white distances and clear air, I resist. In this strange atmosphere, it is sometimes possible to see mountains 300 miles away. And sometimes one can see things that are actually out of sight . . . over the horizon – like a range of hills suddenly rising into view, projected into the sky. It is a phenomenon caused by the refraction of light due to temperature inversion – that is when temperatures at the surface are colder than the air temperature above.

When Shackleton and his companions saw the Beardmore Glacier opening up before them – the first men to set eyes on this gateway to the high polar plateau – they rushed to climb a small, "nearby", 2000-foot mountain of weathered granite in order to survey this possible route to the Pole. It took them seven and a half hours just to reach the foot of the mountain – which they later called Mount Hope – because they, too, had seriously underestimated the distance they needed to go. It is reassuring to be in such good company.

About 16,000 emperor penguin pairs reside on the frozen sea at Amanda Bay, the last rookery accessible to us on the "Far Side". It is also the most spacious and attractive of all ice-bound rookeries. We come in at 500 feet over the sea ice, approaching the shoreline rapidly. High foothills of ice confront the helicopter, but it makes no attempt to rise above them. Instead, it loses altitude and flies down a wide U-shaped valley between the hard, glistening slopes. I realize that what I have mistakenly taken to be the coastline of the continent is simply an offshore barrier of huge, grounded icebergs – the sharpened cone of the highest reaching close to 700 feet. And then, as we land over the waters of the bay, on ice in the early stages of a spring melt, the sense of remoteness, of stillness, of timelessness, is

Emperor and chick. "They are majestic, deliberate, unfailingly formal and elegant – every inch the aristocrat."

almost hypnotic. Behind, the continental ice cap rises steeply away from the shoreline, while to right and left along the arms of the bay, the towering forms of grounded bergs shimmer ambiguously and illusionistically close one moment, distant the next.

The emperors are the largest and most impressive penguins of them all, weighing up to ninety pounds, standing three feet six inches in their slouched position, rising to four feet when fully erect. They are majestic, deliberate, unfailingly formal and elegant – every inch the aristocrat, dressed out in orange, black and white plumage. Their pace is slow, their movements ponderous with their flippers held close in to their sides – yet when they need a burst of speed or are simply tired of walking they fall to their stomachs and toboggan along at up to nine miles per hour. Everything they do is bigger and better than every other penguin. Where most manage to stay submerged for no more than seven minutes, the emperor can stay down for up to eighteen. The maximum depth of dives for most penguins is 230 feet; for the emperor it is 875.

Understandably, a certain mystique has built up around the emperor penguin, as it has, for example, around the wandering albatross – giving rise to all kinds of travellers' tales. Frank Worsley, master of the *Endurance*, recorded the following story on the day before the vessel finally succumbed to the vice-like grip of Weddell Sea ice – her timbers breached and the keel torn out of her: "A strange occurrence was the sudden appearance of eight emperors . . . at the instant the heavy pressure came upon the ship. They walked a little way towards the ship then halted and after a few ordinary cries proceeded to sing what sounded like a dirge for the ship."

Shackleton himself in *South* tells of capturing several emperor penguins earlier in the Weddell Sea and keeping them aboard the *Endurance*. Shortly before the ship was caught in the pack, the birds were released. "They promptly hopped onto the ice, turned around, bowed gracefully and retired to the far side of the floe. There is something curiously human about the manners and movements of these birds. . . ."

Many scientists disapprove of such use of words signifying human traits to interpret animal behaviour. Yet often the only words we possess to illuminate the character of an animal are words created to define our own. Neither should it be forgotten that we, too, are animals and, as such, may have valid insights into the lives of other creatures – who are not themselves without feelings, or conscious awareness of the existential situation, and whose instinctual drives can be modified by some process of reasoning to cope with changes in their external world.

The emperors' breeding habits are unique among Antarctic animals and demand an endurance and discipline that is utterly Spartan. In March, at the onset of winter, the birds congregate on the ice of the rookery to breed. But it is not until May (the equivalent of November in the northern hemisphere) that the female will lay her solitary egg. Then she leaves the rookery, commencing what is often a long dark walk of many miles to the open sea for her first food in two months. Meanwhile the male has taken over the care of the egg, holding it on his feet and protecting it in an overhanging pouch of feathers. The temperature of the egg must never fall below 30°C – whether in the face of gale-force winds or whiteout blizzards with sub-zero temperatures.

The male, to keep from getting snowed in, must move about constantly with the egg held securely on his feet. When the weather becomes especially severe he will join with the other males in a large huddle, this dense grouping helping to conserve heat. Those on the outside slowly work their way toward the centre, those in the middle outward, so each penguin, over time, will share equally in the distribution of heat. For two months the father is the sole responsible parent going without food and losing up to 45 per cent of his body weight before his mate returns to relieve him. Only then will he head off to sea to feed himself.

Yet how benign it all looks on this early summer afternoon beneath a sun warm enough to cause surface melt, with many of the young birds trying to keep cool by breathing through wide open mouths, their flippers spread wide or lying flat on their stomachs stretched out on the ice. These birds – almost ready to go to sea as adults – are the survivors of the winter hatchings. The emperor chick takes six months to reach this point of self-sufficiency – three or four of which are lived under the hardest conditions imaginable – bitter cold, darkness, wind and predation. One estimate of chick mortality puts it as high as 77 per cent during these six gruelling months.

I slog through the thawing ice to the lee of a high humpbacked berg where the emperors are going about their Sunday afternoon capers. I say "capers" in all seriousness because I have never before observed such larking about among the youngsters of a penguin rookery. It seems I have arrived in time to witness the matinée performance of the one and only Amanda Bay *commedia dell' arte.*

This particular section of the rookery comprises a large number of young emperors, resplendent in their soft grey mantles – while dotted around here and there a few adults stand out in startling contrast, the muted grey background of the fledgelings providing a perfect foil for the brilliance of the elders' orange, black and white plumage. The youthful birds are obviously near full grown: they certainly should be with the ice so well into the thaw, the sea almost ready to invite them to start fishing for themselves. But save for one parent assisting its chick by plucking out patches of "baby" hair with its beak, I can see no sign of heavy moulting going on among the remainder of the youthful population – yet if their sea-going feathers are to be exposed ready for the ice-melt, they have little time to spare.

Shuffling away from the colony as I approach – head down and exuding an altogether dejected air – is a young bird closely followed by a stern looking adult whose demeanour is one of universal chastising parenthood: the "Go to your room, young man" sort of look. A domestic drama? The parent urges on its charge with gentle yet firm whacks of its flipper until, on reaching the other end of the rookery, both birds come to a halt. The young penguin shuffles towards its guardian to stand alongside. They are still in the same position half-an-hour later.

Following them has led me to an unusual spectacle. Seven emperor chicks, almost lost to sight, stand in a deep fold of ice at the foot of the grounded iceberg, only their beaks and heads visible below the top of the trench. They are standing in a line, those in the deeper part scarcely able to see out. It is difficult to surmise why they went down there in the first place, unless they were involved in some "follow the leader" kind of game . . . and when the leader slid down the steep and slippery slope at one end of the gully, everybody else piled in behind. In any event, they seem to be accepting the situation quite calmly – even though there is no likely chance of them getting out at the deep end, and hardly any room to manoeuvre and climb out via the shallower, but equally slick, incline at the other. Any escape would depend on the penguin who was last in, and who now must be first out, taking the initiative – a responsibility of which it seems to be blissfully unaware.

OPPOSITE: *Emperor chicks in ice trench. "There they stand, reaching and twisting to try and peer over the rim like a platoon of soldiers in a trench."*

There they stand, reaching and twisting to try and peer over the rim like a platoon of soldiers in a trench. It is necessary for them to get out in case the comparatively warm air gives way to cold, turning the only escape route into glass. It is, of course, possible that they really like "being in the groove" as it were – find the enclosure a satisfying change after spending months on the windswept flats above. In any event, there isn't much to do about their predicament – save keep an eye on the situation.

Meanwhile, penguin life at the heart of the rookery is proceeding normally: the more settled youngsters wait patiently, as returning parents come plodding homeward, heads thrust forward, making straight for their patient offspring.

This peaceful domestic scene is interrupted by an anarchic mob of slightly older chicks – or so they seem, being larger than the rest and less interested in standing around to be fed. They come waddling out from hidden regions between the grounded bergs and begin to mill around on the left flank of the central group. At some point – after a certain minimal order is achieved – they begin to march up a narrow ledge projecting from the iceberg which protects the community. At the highest point they are probably thirty feet above the heads of the less adventurous penguins beneath them. There is a certain amount of jostling going on as the procession makes its way aloft, birds coming dangerously close to the edge yet managing always to keep from tumbling off.

I do not have long to wait before the object of the exercise becomes clear. At its high point the ledge levels out and continues around the sloping side of the berg for about forty-five feet before terminating in a natural chute – the only way down to the ground. The first half of this slide falls steeply, levels out briefly in the middle of the run, then slopes more gently downward to the ground.

It is obvious what is about to happen. On arriving at the end of the trail, the drop-off before them, the chicks launch themselves one after another down the chute like children in a playground. Some go down on both legs, flippers extended, like accomplished skiers; others abandon their bodies to gravity and descend on their backs or on their fronts, head first. Apart from some shoving at the top of the slide from those eager to jump

OPPOSITE: *The slide. "… the group now gathered at the bottom decide they want to try it again and begin to take the short route back to the top …"*

the queue, the operation goes pretty smoothly until the group now gathered at the bottom decide they want to try it again and begin to take the short route back to the top – which, of course, means scaling the chute itself. One after the other they start up, only to be bowled over by those still coming down. Some actually make it to the middle section of the run, where they bond together as a furry grey wall to oppose those on top still planning to come down. This living barrier survives two onslaughts . . . and then all are swept downhill like a row of ninepins.

At the base of the slide they try to sort themselves out. Meanwhile the line of those waiting at the top is as long as ever, and clearly no one up there thinks of waiting for things on the ground to settle down before launching into the downhill run. Neither does the group at the bottom do very much about clearing space for those about to come down. On the contrary – several obvious slow learners still persist in trying to climb to the top and rejoin the line above.

Then, quite abruptly, the exercise is abandoned. For no apparent reason, youngsters just stand wherever they happen to be, as if they have been playing a variation of musical chairs, surveying the local scene. When I leave them a few minutes later to return to the penguins in the ice gully, the former skiers are still in the positions as before. The ledge detachment remains in line on the heights making no attempt to descend; the two or three birds who have attained the slide's mid-section stay put, as does the party at the base. Everybody just hanging out, just taking the air, as it were. It seems that, for some reason totally unperceived by me, suddenly enough was enough.

On returning to the ice gully, I am fascinated to see that six of the young emperors have escaped from the imprisoning cleft – standing around apparently uncertain as to what to do next. They must have come out at the shallow end, yet I cannot imagine how they negotiated the long and almost vertical wall of hard ice.

The seventh bird alone remains trapped. As I consider ways in which I might help it, the chick moves rapidly of its own volition. Hastening to the low end of the trench, it starts up the slippery ramp. Using its pronounced and strong beak like an ice pick, the chick pulls itself, stage by stage, up the formidable incline, though not without some difficulty: every time the youngster releases its beak from the ice to dig in at a higher level, it begins to slide. It overcomes this problem and avoids falling by pressing into the corner of the exit face and the trench wall, enabling itself to use two

The blue crèche. "… once out it wastes no time setting off immediately at a calm and measured pace to rejoin its companions now standing on a hillock of ice a short distance away."

surfaces to provide purchase for its flailing feet and flippers. It is a gallant yet exhausting effort requiring frequent rests – short periods when the bird clings to the walls supported only by its anchored beak.

Five minutes pass before it finally hauls itself on to the level surface of the sea ice. But once out it wastes no time setting off immediately at a calm and measured pace to rejoin its companions now standing on a hillock of ice a short distance away.

Were they waiting for their last colleague to escape the gully? Who knows? All I can say is that as soon as number seven joins them, the group moves off.

I take a last look around. Groups of penguins assume the aspect of characters in a painting – small studies of penguin life captured and scattered across the canvas, detached from the overall scene. These little

Emperor tableau. "These little vignettes become cameos by Pieter Brueghel, paintings of Flemish penguin-peasants going stiffly about their business in the depths of a northern winter."

vignettes become cameos by Pieter Brueghel, paintings of Flemish penguin-peasants going stiffly about their business in the depths of a northern winter. The characters shift, even leave the painting for a while. But, as in any great work of art, the scene endures as a timeless tableau. New generations come in to replace the old, but nothing of the Antarctic backdrop changes. Against the harsh round of the seasons – the darkness of winter and the brilliance of summer – the gallant birds move in and out as they seem to have been doing from the beginning of time.

I remind myself on climbing into the helicopter that here at Amanda Bay – at 69° 20′ – we have reached our own furthest south to be realized on this voyage.

THE CALL OF THE
LITTLE VOICES

"What is this fascination with the ice, then . . . ?"

The question is usually asked in a bemused kind of way, and is one I have never been able to respond to briefly or casually. The interrogator, who expects Antarctica to be revealed in its essence by a two-minute travel-brochure presentation, will be out of luck. But on those occasions when I perceive myself to be in the presence of a potential convert, I grab my inquisitor by the arm in true Ancient Mariner style, and lead him or her to some quiet corner. There, struggling with language like some "arthritic wrestler", as Dylan Thomas put it, I try to convey something of the revelatory change which comes over one when venturing into these regions.

For myself, it was first a matter of realizing that here was a place where the only indigenous life-forms were some rock lichen and the odd Antarctic flea – that this massive continent of ice-bound bedrock had not brought forth a single human being. It was a *tabula rasa* so far as any human history or ethos was concerned. I suspect that it was for this reason that my own long-held and comfortable philosophy of life, fostered by western, middle-class values, involuntarily retreated – it suddenly seemed shallow, lacking in profundity.

As the days passed, so the feeling of being adrift – physically and mentally – intensified. The surreal quality imposed by the light and surrounding variety of ice-forms, the loss of a sense of time and the knowledge of one's supreme isolation at the bottom of the world, added further to confound all impressions of normality. I found myself beset by the vague unease which comes from a constant subliminal awareness of danger – the unpredictability inherent in such a harsh and elementally violent environment.

Yet this general uncertainty results in a sharpening of perceptions: the arrival of a higher level of awareness which exposes the triviality of much that goes on in our lives – trivialities which the place demands be shed. A new dialogue starts within oneself in which the eye speaks eloquently to the mind, and the mind equally eloquently to that interior arbiter we call the spirit. One is pushed to confront the essential mystery presented by all awesome phenomena – "why?" and "to what end?"

In facing the reality of these extreme southern latitudes – even vicariously – it is not possible to avoid acknowledging and contemplating the coldest reality the world has to offer: the brevity and frailty of life for us all – us and the albatross together.

Frank Wild, that great unsung hero of Antarctic exploration, talked about "a sort of wandering lostness" which he experienced in the Antarctic, in the light of which civilisation was artificial and unsightly; that he had seen "the most materialistic and unimpressionable of men strung to an absolute silence . . . the very sledge dogs stand stock still, gazing intently into the farness, ears cocked, listening – for what?" When asked why he would risk everything by going yet again to the ice at the edge of the world – after surviving so many dangers and privations, he replied, "Once you have been to the white unknown, you can never escape the call of the little voices."

I hope I have managed to convey something of their potency.

East Antarctic tone poem. "Once you have been to the white unknown, you can never escape the call of the little voices."

Appendix A

AMUNDSEN, Roald: Norwegian. [1872–1928]

1905: First to navigate the Northwest Passage in an old fishing boat, the *Gjoa*. 1911: First to reach the South Pole. On 14 January 1911 Amundsen set up his Base Camp on the Ross Ice Shelf in the Bay of Whales, and set off for the South Pole on 20 October 1911 with four companions and twelve dogs per sled. They crossed the Ross Ice Shelf (the Barrier) and pioneered the ascent of the Axel Heiberg Glacier to reach the high Polar Plateau. They reached the Pole on 14 December. There Amundsen left a letter for Scott which the Englishman was to find a month later. The Norwegian team were back at their "Framheim" Base on 25 January 1912. The round trip was accomplished in just ninety-six days.
1926: In the airship *Norge*, Amundsen, with Ellsworth and Nobile, were the first to fly to the North Pole.
1928: On 18 June, Amundsen was lost flying with four companions in an attempt to locate survivors of the *Italia*, an airship which crashed on its return from reaching the North Pole.

BELLINGSHAUSEN, Thaddeus von: Captain, Imperial Russian Navy. [1778–1852]

1819–1821: Made a noteworthy circumnavigation of the Antarctic continent with two ships, sailing round the Southern Ocean in a clockwise direction, completing his voyage in the sea that now bears his name and in which he discovered Peter I Island.

BORCHGREVINK, Carsten: Norwegian. [1864–1934]

1899: His expedition, in the ship *Southern Cross*, was the first to winter-over in Antarctica. His

pioneering base was on the Robertson Bay side of Cape Adare in Victoria Land, in the region where Commander Campbell together with Sir Raymond Priestley of Scott's Northern Party wintered in 1911; after which they were forced to winter-over yet again in the more southern reaches of Victoria Land.

BOWERS, Henry: Lieutenant, Royal Indian Marine. [1883–1912]

1910–13: An indefatigable and all-round tower of strength in Scott's *Terra Nova* expedition. A short man of great physical strength, he was capable of withstanding pain and privation to extraordinary degrees. Highly competent as a seaman and capable of swift action to avert catastrophe. Much respected and liked by all members of the expedition. Together with Apsley Cherry-Garrard and Edward Wilson he set out on the Winter Journey to Cape Crozier from Cape Evans in order to obtain – for scientific reasons – the first emperor penguin eggs from a winter-breeding colony. On 1 November 1911, a bare three months later, he left Cape Evans with Scott and the rest of the Southern Party en route to the South Pole. He died in the tent with Scott and Wilson on or about 19 March 1912.

CHERRY-GARRARD, Apsley: Youngest member of Scott's scientific team. [1886–1959]

1910–13: Independently wealthy, he contributed financially to the expedition. Wrote *The Worst Journey in the World* describing the horrors and hazards of the Winter Journey to Cape Crozier. He took part in the search for the Polar Party over the Barrier in November 1912, and discovered the bodies of Scott, Wilson and Bowers in their tent.

ABOVE: *Wilson, Bowers and Cherry-Garrard on their return from Cape Crozier.*

BELOW: *Mawson's expedition party in their hut. Mawson is standing on the left.*

MAWSON, Sir Douglas: Australian. [1882–1958]
1908–09: Member of Ernest Shackleton's *Nimrod*
expedition at Cape Royds. Member of Edgeworth David's
party sledging northward in Victoria Land to locate the
elusive south magnetic pole.
1911–13: After declining to join Scott's last expedition he
led his own *Aurora* expedition to explore the unknown
regions west of Cape Adare as far as the ice shelf he
named after Shackleton. He established his base at Cape
Denison, Commonwealth Bay. He later wrote *The Land of
the Blizzard* in which the accomplishments and tragedies
(his loss of Ninnis and Mertz and his own solitary and
brutal journey back to Cape Denison) are described.
1929–31: Made the two voyages of exploration around the
coast of East Antarctica in Scott's old vessel *Discovery*, which
established British-Australian influence on the "Far Side".

OATES, Lawrence, nicknamed "Titus": Captain, 5th Royal
Inniskilling Dragoon Guards. [1880–1912] Saw service in
the Boer War in South Africa. Excellent horseman and
trainer of horses.
1910–13: Joined Scott's *Terra Nova* expedition to be in charge
of the ponies which were to pull the sleds. (Scott selected
ponies rather than dogs for sled hauling.) He frequently
pointed out to Scott the poor condition of the animals for the
job in hand. He suffered greatly on the return from the Pole
from the steadily increasing gangrenous condition of both
feet. In temperatures of –43°F he struggled on, obstinately
defying death and refusing to take the thirty opium tablets

which would have eased his dying: this was not a soldierly
solution – and Oates was not referred to simply as "Soldier"
for nothing. On 15 March 1912, with advanced frostbite on
hands and feet, paralyzed by pain and knowing what a
hindrance he was to the party's progress, he resolved to die.
As death was approaching too slowly, he simply went out to
meet it. Uttering those now famous words, "I am just going
outside and I may be some time," he went out into a raging
blizzard. He was not seen again.

ROSS, Sir James Clark: Captain, Royal Navy. [1800–62]
Prior to 1839 Ross had distinguished himself on several
Arctic voyages, on one of which he had attained the
northern magnetic pole.
1839–43: Over these four years Ross made three Antarctic
voyages with two ice-strengthened wooden ships, *Erebus*
and *Terror*. On the first voyage he discovered Cape Adare.
Continuing to sail south he arrived in the large bay which
he named McMurdo. The island now known as Ross
Island lay alongside, Mount Erebus smoking away.
Leaving McMurdo and sailing east he found himself
following the 500-mile wall of ice now known as the
Barrier. Historically called the Ross Ice Shelf, it floats in
the sea named the Ross Sea. On the second voyage Ross
set out to explore the great ice shelf he had discovered but
very bad weather turned them back to Tasmania. His
intention on the third voyage was to pursue yet another
route south, but by March 1843 the season was too far
advanced for him to proceed beyond 71°30′ south.

Captain Oates with the ponies on the Terra Nova

Sir James Clark Ross

Scott and party at the South Pole

SCOTT, Robert Falcon: Captain, Royal Navy.[1868–1912]
1902–03: First Polar expedition – in the specially built ship *Discovery* – to explore the possibility of reaching the South Pole. Reached "furthest south" over the Barrier but did not ascend to the high Polar Plateau.
1911–13: The *Terra Nova* expedition which reached the South Pole a month after Amundsen. The party had been out on the ice for almost four months; the weather was unbelievably hostile; and the surviving three members died in the tent on the return about 150 miles from base.

SHACKLETON, Sir Ernest: British Merchant Marine Officer. [1874–1922]
1902–03: Member of Scott's First Polar expedition to

reach "furthest south". Invalided home suffering from scurvy.
1908–09: Led his own *Nimrod* Polar expedition. Established base at Cape Royds. Mawson and Priestley were expedition members. By the end of November 1908 Shackleton had beaten Scott's "furthest south" record, discovered the Beardmore Glacier and gained access to the Polar Plateau. Turned back when some 97 nautical miles from the Pole due to the violent weather and their worsening physical condition.
1914–16: *Endurance* expedition. The Weddell Sea disaster; the long sojourn on the sea ice; the three small boats battering their way to Elephant Island loaded to the gunwales; Shackleton's famous small boat journey in the

Ernest Shackleton, at the age of 47

James Caird to South Georgia; the crossing of the Allardyce Range; and ultimately the rescue of the men left on Elephant Island.

1922: In the early hours of 5 January, aboard the *Quest* and heading south yet again, Shackleton died. He, Worsley and Wild had sighted South Georgia the previous afternoon. He was buried on the island that saw the culmination of his greatest triumph.

WILD, Frank: Commander, Royal Navy. [1873–1939]
1908–09: With Shackleton on the *Nimrod* expedition. A tireless and "unflappable" aide to Shackleton on the perilous return from the aborted Pole journey.
1911–13: With Mawson on the *Aurora* expedition based at Cape Denison. Leader of the Western Party whose camp was on the Shackleton Ice Shelf. In terrible weather conditions Wild and his team surveyed hundreds of miles of coastline.
1914–16: Second-in-command to Shackleton on the

Commander Wild at the masthead

Endurance expedition, and in charge of the men left on Elephant Island. Kept discipline and morale at a high level during the months before rescue arrived.
1922–23: Took over the *Quest*'s scientific brief in the Southern Ocean after Shackleton's death and completed the work. He was devoted to "the Boss", and his life later ended tragically in South Africa. Without Shackleton and the ice and his "little voices" it would seem he was lost.

Dr Wilson

Frank Worsley

WILSON, Edward: Doctor, naturalist, and artist.
[1872–1912]
1902–03: With Scott on the First Polar expedition which reached "furthest south".
1910–13: Led the terrible winter journey to Cape Crozier from Scott's McMurdo base to collect emperor penguin eggs for scientific research. Always took on the most hazardous lead position on this fearsome trek. Three months later he was off with Scott to the South Pole. Died on the return and was found in the tent with Bowers and Scott. A man both loved and respected by his colleagues. He gave help and advice whenever it was required. The recognized "wise one" of the expedition. His notes and colour sketches of Antarctic wildlife are renowned, both for their scientific observation and their artistic fineness.

WORSLEY, Frank: Commander of *Endurance*.
[1872–1943]
1914–16: Shackleton's master mariner on the *Endurance* expedition. Excellent seaman and navigator. Took the *James Caird* to South Georgia across 800 miles of a wintry Southern Ocean with very few sextant shots at a sun appearing but infrequently, and those from a tossing small boat. Accompanied Shackleton across South Georgia's Allardyce Range. Like Frank Wild he believed in Shackleton and gave of himself unflinchingly to the cause of the expedition. After the rescue of the men on Elephant Island he returned to England and commanded a destroyer in the final years of the First World War.

Appendix B

FURTHER READING AND BOOKS MENTIONED IN THE TEXT

BAINBRIDGE, Beryl
The Birthday Boys. Carroll & Graf, NewYork, 1991.

BICKEL, Leonard
Mawson's Will. Stein & Day, New York, 1977.

BODINGTON, Jennie
1910–1916 Antarctic Photographs, Herbert Ponting & Frank Hurley – Scott, Mawson and Shackleton Expeditions. St. Martin's Press, New York, 1979.

CAMPBELL, Victor
The Wicked Mate: Antarctic Diary of Victor Campbell. Edited by H. G. R. King. Bluntisham Books, Erskine Press, Aldburgh, Norfolk, 1988

CHERRY-GARRARD, Apsley
The Worst Journey In the World: Antarctic 1910–1913. Carroll & Graf, New York/Chatto & Windus, London, 1965.

FOGG, G. E. and SMITH, David
The Exploration of Antarctica. Cassell, London, 1990.

HALLE, Louis J.
The Sea and the Ice. Cornell University Press, 1973.

HAMBREY, Michael and ALEAN, Jürg
Glaciers. Cambridge University Press, 1992.

HUNTFORD, Roland
Shackleton. Hodder and Stoughton, London, 1985.

HUNTFORD, Roland
Scott and Amundsen – The Race to the South Pole. Hodder and Stoughton, London, 1979.

HURLEY, Frank
Argonauts of the South. G. P. Putnam's Sons, New York, 1925.

KING, H. G. R.
The Antarctic. Blandford Press, London, 1969.

LANSING, Alfred
Endurance. McGraw Hill, New York, 1959: new edn Carroll & Graf, New York, 1999.

LIMB, Sue and CORDINGLEY, Patrick
Captain Oates: Soldier & Explorer. B. T. Batsford, London, 1982.

MAWSON, Sir Douglas
The Home of the Blizzard – Being the Story of the Australasian Antarctic Expedition, 1911–1914. William Heinemann, London, 1915.

MIGOT, André
Thin Edge of the World. Little, Brown, Boston, 1956.

PONTING, Herbert G.
The Great White South. Gerald Duckworth, London, 1921.

PRICE, A. Grenfell
The Winning of Australian Antarctica – Mawson's B.A.N.Z.A.R.E. Voyages, 1929–1931. Angus & Robertson, Sydney, 1962.

PRIESTLEY, Sir Raymond E.
Antarctic Adventure: Scott's Northern Party. T. Fisher Unwin, London, 1914.

RAWLING, Christopher
Shackleton: His Antarctic Writings – Selected & Introduced. British Broadcasting Corporation, London, 1983.

ROSS, M. J.
Ross in the Antarctic. Caedmon of Whitby Publishers, Whitby, 1982.

SEAVER, G.
'Birdie' Bowers of the Antarctic. John Murray, London, 1938.

SEAVER, G.
Edward Wilson of the Antarctic. John Murray, London, 1936.

SHACKLETON, Sir Ernest
South. Carroll & Graf, New York/Robinson, London, 1998.

STONEHOUSE, Bernard
Animals of the Antarctic: The Ecology of the South. Holt, Rinehart, New York, 1972.

WORSLEY, Frank Arthur
Shackleton's Board Journey. W. & W. Norton, New York, 1977.

WORSLEY, Frank Arthur
Endurance: An Epic of Polar Adventure. Jonathan Cape and Harrison Smith, New York, 1931.

The Antarctic Pilot. Hydrographic Department, London, 1961.

Reader's Digest: Antarctica – The Extraordinary History of Man's Conquest of the Frozen Continent. Reader's Digest (Australia) Pty Limited, Surrey Hills, New South Wales, 1990.

South Polar Times Volume III – April–October 1911. Smith, Elder, London, 1914.

Index